301110 5062548 1

GW00685154

the architecture of the jubilee line extension

David Bennett with photographs by Dennis Gilbert

Thomas Telford

Published by Thomas Telford Publishing, Thomas Telford Ltd, 1 Heron Quay, London E14 4JD.
www.thomastelford.com

Distributors for Thomas Telford books are
USA: ASCE Press, 1801 Alexander Bell Drive, Reston, VA 20191-4400, USA
Japan: Maruzen Co. Ltd, Book Department, 3–10 Nihonbashi 2-chome, Chuo-ku, Tokyo 103
Australia: DA Books and Journals, 648 Whitehorse Road, Mitcham 3132, Victoria

First published 2004

Also available from Thomas Telford Books
The Jubilee Line Extension, B. Mitchell, 2003. ISBN 0 7277 3028 2.
The architecture of bridge design, D. Bennett, 1997. ISBN 0 7277 2529 7.
Innovations in concrete, D. Bennett, 2002. ISBN 0 7277 2005 8.

Dennis Gilbert's pictures appear courtesy of:

VIEW Pictures, 14 The Dove Centre, 109 Bartholomew Rd, London NW5 2BJ United Kingdom
tel +44 20 7284 2928   fax +44 20 7284 3617   www.viewpictures.co.uk

Copies of the photographs may be obtained from VIEW for publication or display.

A catalogue record for this book is available from the British Library

ISBN: 0 7277 3088 6

Designed and typeset by Kneath Associates
Printed and bound in Great Britain by CUP

the architecture of the jubilee line extension

Contents

Foreword

David Bennett

From the outset London Transport's former Chairman, Sir Wilfred Newton, and Managing Director, Denis Tunnicliffe, were in firm agreement that the new Jubilee Line Extension (JLE) should divorce itself as far as possible from the traditional feel of the existing underground system. This approach led to the conscious decision to use architects to lead the design strategy for both the stations and the new depot at Stratford.

It was proposed that each of the eleven stations should be designed as individual entities, linked to one another by a common philosophy. Roland Paoletti was invited to be the overall architect manager of the JLE, with an in-house team of architects to carry out detailed design work and site management duties, and to make the external appointments of architects for each station. There were pragmatic reasons for spreading the workload, as there was going to be very little time to produce the full working drawings required for tender.

Left on their own, civil engineers, it seems, will all too easily take on board architects with whom they feel socially comfortable and who would probably conform rather than question their approach to design. The results of this, more often than not, are underground stations with labyrinthine tunnels and formless spaces – utility and economy of scale overriding passenger comfort, ease of movement, visual clarity and context. This was not the approach taken by Paoletti.

The policy he adopted for the JLE stations was to allow free rein to some of the country's leading architects in order to find bold and elegant design solutions. When the architects and their design concepts were first publicised in September 1992 they met with universal approval. But nothing was achieved without a lot of hard work, frustration, grudging respect and understanding between the civil engineering overlords and their architect partners. Most of the station designs were a compromise between

the pragmatism of civil engineering and the imaginative flair of the architect. What the architects were striving to do was to express the art of deep excavation construction and tunnelling, and introduce light-filled, liberating spaces. What the civil engineers were very afraid of was that the architects would add extra cost and complication to the enterprise and, with their love of publicity, steal all the glory. To date, not one of the civil engineering consultants who worked on the stations has had a bad word to say about their architect partners.

Now the stations are open we can all see how the architects have redefined the use of underground space. They have helped to produce stations that respond to passenger movement, that will meet the long-term spatial needs of increased usage and above all integrate well with their external location. But it has to be said that not all of them are an architectural *tour de force*. Some architects were given a very minimal budget to work with e.g. West

Ham, Canning Town and the Stratford platforms. Only a select few were really allowed to express the architecture as they saw fit – Canary Wharf, Westminster, North Greenwich and Stratford Terminus. Opinions will differ as to what is good architecture and whether the design team have kept faithfully to the brief they were given. A section at the end of the book gives two personal reflections on what aspects of the JLE stations have been impressive and what have not lived up to their expectations five years after the line has been opened. These are subjective views and have been introduced to help the reader make up their own mind about what pleases them. It is not to be read as a criticism of the architects themselves, all of whom have taken great care and integrity in the approach to their work.

Only station buildings and structures that can be seen during a tube journey are considered in this book. Stratford Market Depot, the ventilation shafts which can be visited and the interlinking bus stations (which are very accessible and exciting structures in their own right) are not covered in any depth, although they get a brief mention.

The commentary on each station has been written and edited by the author after detailed discussion with the architect(s) concerned. Those who were interviewed or provided the background text have been named under the station heading. In many instances the text that was provided was so well written it hardly needed tinkering with. The rough sketches, preliminary concept drawings and architectural illustrations that accompany each station show how the organisation of underground spaces evolved and how the surfaces were profiled and detailed to compliment the civil engineering of its construction. The monumental forms of tunnel segments, bracing ties, diaphragm walls, supporting columns and roof canopies (and other characteristics of deep excavations generally hidden from view) are revealed for the first time to become the architecture's dynamic. The quality of the finished stations and the sense of space that it conveys once again reminds us that architecture must become an integral part of all major transport undertakings and infrastructure design, to ensure that we have some semblance of clarity and order in the built environment of tomorrow.

I am indebted to Roland Paoletti for the time he has devoted to discussing the background research to this book. I am extremely grateful to all those architects who gave of their time and talked so openly and freely about aspects of the architecture and engineering of their stations. But the really big thanks and deepest gratitude must go to Dennis Gilbert for the photography that he has specially taken for this book in black and white. His sensitive and intelligent camerawork brings out the real character of the architecture of each station and says much more than all the words in the text. His photography has transformed the illustrative quality of this book from merely interesting to visually stunning and engagingly captivating.

An overview of the JLE design strategy

Roland Paoletti CBE - Head of Architecture and Station Design, Jubilee Line Extension Project

In early 1990 I was invited by London Underground to be responsible for the design of the sequence of stations of the Jubilee Line Extension. Within two years, by 1992, using a combination of high calibre London architects and a specially recruited team of my own, the designs of the eleven stations and great depot were essentially done. I was brought from Hong Kong for this. There I had been chief architect for the Mass Transit Railway, mainly involved in the huge commercial developments above the stations and depots. Before that, I had spent a number of years with the great Italian engineer Pier Luigi Nervi, the combination of these experiences providing an extraordinarily apt education for the task on the Jubilee Line.

It was firmly expected that, following the Hong Kong precedent, a single unified theme would be designed for all the stations on the basis of conventional engineering solutions. Before I left Hong Kong, however, I had already resolved to propose otherwise and after some months of delay this was agreed. In short, my proposal was that each of the eleven stations of the JLE should be designed as an individual entity, but linked to the others by an

underlying philosophy and essential elements. Each should be unique and contribute strongly to the neighbourhood while at the same time representing recognisably the best of London Underground. Some stations should have more money spent on them than others. A different London architect should be chosen for each station and depot.

There were solid philosophical and practical reasons for spreading the load. A single architect would be too vulnerable and tend to iron things out. In this case, in the very short time that we had given ourselves to produce drawings for construction, it would have been difficult to achieve the high-quality results and variety I was seeking without the use of a number of architects.

In 1990 the response from the architects to advertisements for engineering and architectural consultants interested in designing the JLE and its stations was both sparse and disappointing, in spite of the fact that there was a recession and little architectural work about. The extension of a 1970s underground line, that

itself had been cobbled together from older lines, across ten unprepossessing miles of east and south-east London was simply not an interesting proposal for the architectural profession. Moreover, visits to and talks with many architects exposed their further doubts, which were partly to do with civil engineering management and partly with the architecture of earlier tube lines. Nevertheless, the intrinsic potential of the extension was explained to them and they were told that if they were not then able to help, it really would be the end as far as authentic architecture and the underground railway was concerned.

Preference was not given to 'transport' architects, as to do so would have excluded many of the most capable architects in the metropolis. No architect was selected on reputation alone. Like-minded architects were sought who, it was thought, would do the job well and possessed the talent for understanding the engineering. In short, they were chosen as a loose team with strong characteristics stemming from a common enthusiasm for and knowledge of engineering and, individually, an aptitude for resolution of the problems particular to each station.

In my experience, underground engineers either provide the spatial layouts themselves or all too easily take on board pliable designers with whom they feel comfortable. This often produces labyrinthine tunnels and ad-hoc formless spaces usually encrusted with some mild decoration as a palliative. By contrast, on the JLE, an open-minded commissioning policy, that gave some of the country's best architects free rein to challenge civil engineering preconceptions and allowed them to work on the stations in their entirety, from the street to platform levels, has been rewarded with a highly functional series of bold and intelligent designs.

Together with the concept of achieving a symbiosis of architecture and engineering – with daylight itself used as a structuring device – the design priorities were to provide generous and easily understood space, clear and direct passenger routing, a sufficiency of escalators (a total of 118 increasing the number in the network by over 40 per cent), lifts for the disabled and safety in all aspects, particularly by the provision of protected escape routes. Priority was given to providing those elements, that can

never be introduced once a station is built, rather than elaborate finishes. Indeed, instruction was given to leave the civil work exposed wherever possible, to un-decorate rather than decorate the station.

In the end, the architects' considerable contribution has been a re-examination of what engineers do, in an effort to return to the origins of engineering. They have defined space and re-invented it.

When I was asked to give a talk to the Major Projects' Association in 2000 about the achievement of the JLE, I wrote the following as an introduction:

'It is impossible to imagine two more inflexible cultures than those of heavy railways and infrastructural engineering. An underground railway has both. The JLE's extraordinary achievement has been to break with a tradition of design conformity, developed and consolidated for over a century, and create something of exceptional quality from something so ordinary as the tail end of an existing tube line. What the Extension

managed extraordinarily to do was to create a situation that allowed heavy engineering, which is so often static and inhuman, and locked in an unbreakable pattern of unchanging and unchangeable solutions, to become instead, resourceful and brilliant and active in response to architectural initiatives.'

To what end you may ask? Early in my career I spent several years as one of Pier Luigi Nervi's small team working from Rome on buildings in various parts of the world. I accompanied that great engineer to London in 1968, when he was given the Institution of Structural Engineers Gold Medal, to help with the interviews. A year later he gave the final lecture of his long life, at which he was awarded the Feltrinelli Prize for Architecture – in this he lauded at length, as was his wont, the principles and practicalities of construction and its economies but, nevertheless, ended it by emphasising that there was more to it than that. For Nervi – and for me – 'the only end to which architecture can and must aspire is that of providing a serious background to people's lives, one that contributes to the education of serious men'.

one

© **Westminster** Architect: Michael Hopkins and Partners

David Selby, Michael Hopkins and Partners
John Pringle, Pringle Richards Sharratt Architects (formerly of Michael Hopkins)

The story of the station began with the brief from Parliament for new office accommodation, well before we were commissioned for the underground station. Parliament had a real need for new accommodation for their MPs, some of whom occupied offices without windows perched on the roofs of the Palace of Westminster. The site at Bridge Street, around the station, was one of the few sites within the area available to Parliament. It had, however, enormous complications – an old cut-and-cover underground station with tracks running diagonally across the site at a little more than one storey below street level, and close to the historic buildings that front onto Bridge Street. The buildings on the site were occupied mainly by Parliament and although they were considered attractive, their French mansard roofs were in very bad condition.

escalator and tubular
bracing

schematic drawing

Various redevelopment and retention options for the site
were produced for consideration by Parliament. All
these schemes were constrained by the compromise of
retaining the existing buildings and the existing station.
It was not until the Jubilee Line Extension Bill was
passed by Parliament that a more rational approach for
comprehensive redevelopment became a possibility.

Our appointment as architects for the new station and a
new building created a real opportunity for an integrated
solution for the Westminster site. The challenge was to
weave the requirements of both the building and the
station together into one. Each area demanded a
different solution and from that developed different
structural forms and spatial qualities. The real prize was
to create a ground floor courtyard for the Parliamentary
building at street level while inserting a whole new
storey for the much-needed new ticket offices between

plan: ticket hall level

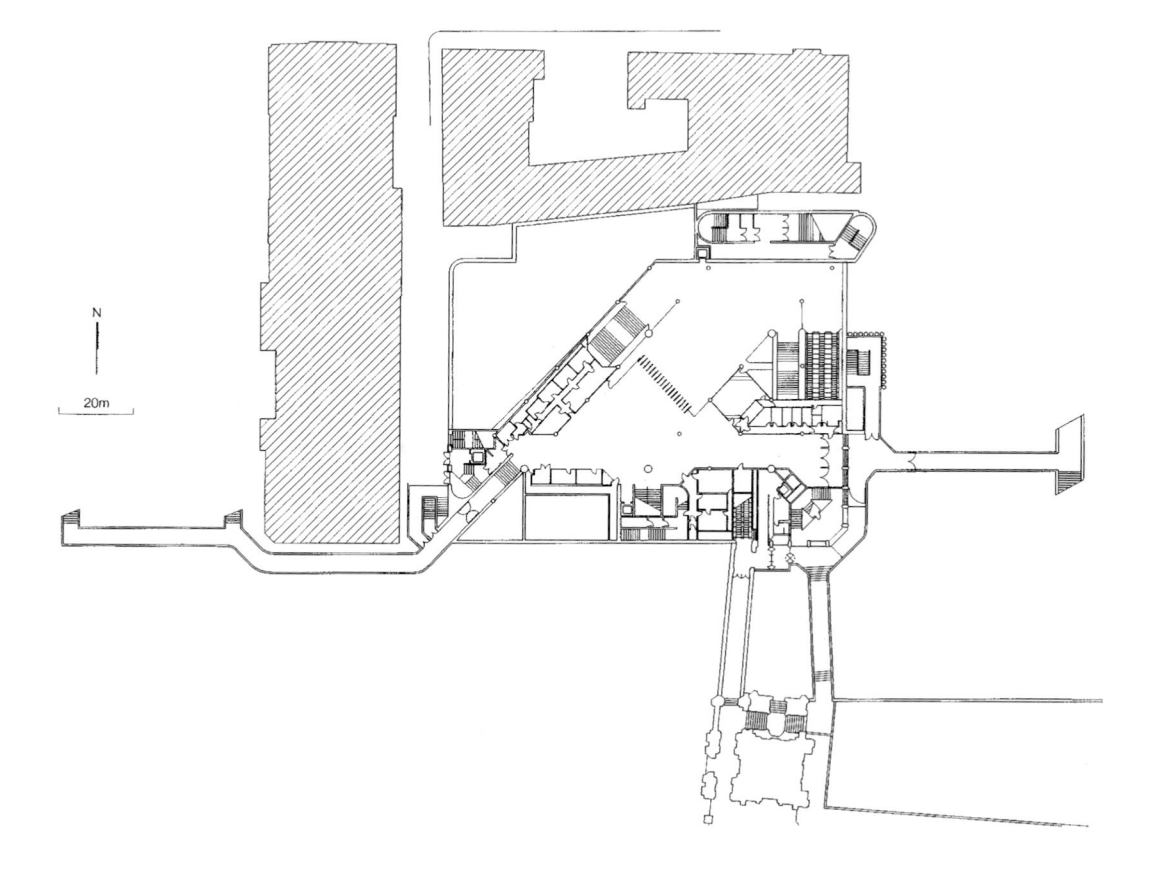

N

20m

Our appointment as architects for the new station and a new building created a real opportunity for an integrated solution for the Westminster site. The challenge was to weave the requirements of both the building and the station together into one.

street level and the level of the existing underground tracks. By designing the new Parliamentary building to incorporate arched transfer structures around a new courtyard and by lowering the existing tracks of the District and Circle Line slightly, it was possible for both the ticket hall and platform levels to be sandwiched between the track and the building above it. The complications of the existing configuration of diagonal tracks were another major challenge, which translated into a diagonal grid of beams called 'diagrids' to support the floors above the existing configurations of the tracks. As a result the ticket hall and the District and Circle Line have a very flat, horizontal spatial quality and connect by means of extensive subways to the adjacent streets.

The next challenge was to connect the ticket hall and the District and Circle Line platforms to the new JLE

tunnels. At Westminster the JLE tunnels are stacked vertically rather than the more usual side-by-side arrangement. This was done in order to reduce settlement effects upon Big Ben and Westminster Bridge and to avoid having to support the new Parliamentary building above. Usually connections to platforms are made by escalators within bored tunnels, but at Westminster the constrained site and the need to co-ordinate the structures of the buildings and station made it desirable to create a large escalator hall, which became known as the 'box'.

The volume required for the intersecting escalators to carry people on their way to the platforms is huge. The escalator 'box' is 72 m long, 22 m wide and 30 m deep below ground – as much as the height of the new building above ground. To resist the forces of the ground around the escalator box a massive structure was

required. A grid of wide beams and columns restrain a perimeter 'diaphragm' wall, which was cast against the earth and clay giving it a very rough cliff-like appearance. The grid of wide beams and columns are themselves kept apart by horizontal struts of solid steel, which also support the escalators like a series of suspended walkways, weaving their way through a huge Piranesian cavern.

Our architectural approach was to reveal this massive structure, the bones of the station (which was created under incredibly difficult conditions) – without covering it up by false linings or finishes – to show it warts and all. The noise of moving escalators, with their steel supports and precise machine-like details, gives the whole space the feeling of a huge engine room. As it enters the escalator box, the diagonal escalator connection from the level of the District and Circle Line platforms is quite

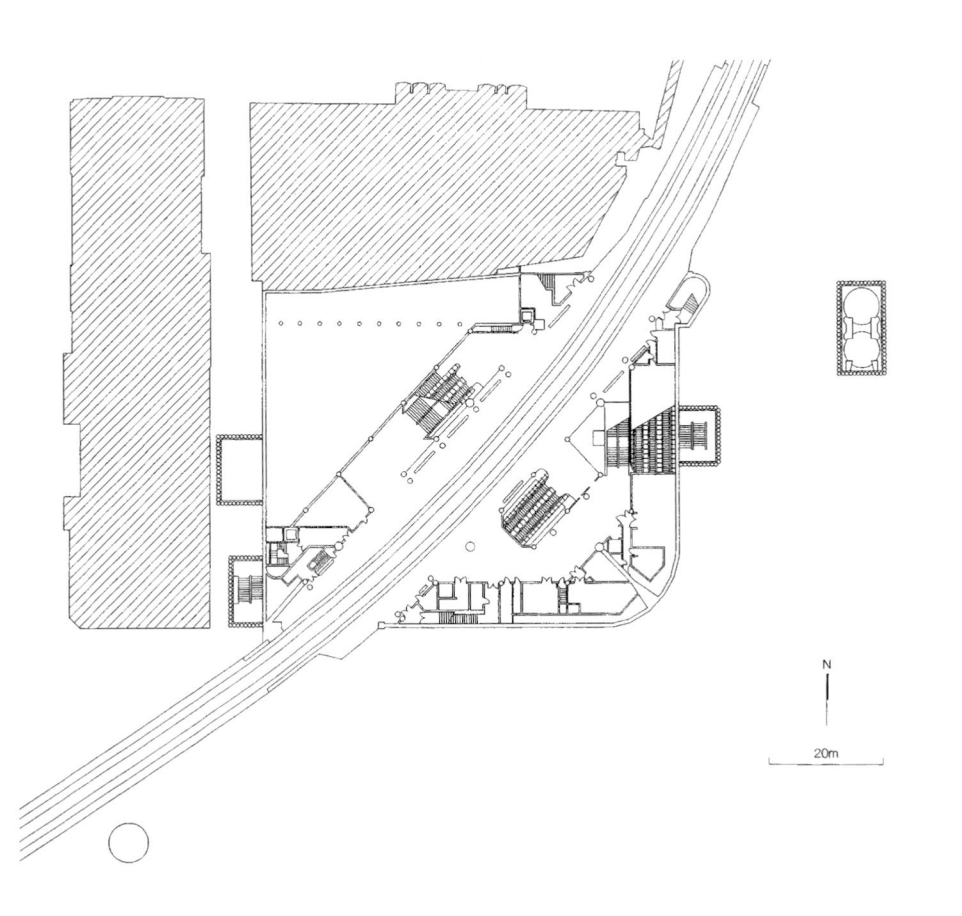

N

20m

column and bracing

The materials of the civil engineering structure form a rugged backdrop for the hierarchy of finished elements such as escalators and acoustically absorptive surfaces.

breathtaking, with diagonal views of moving escalators and people against the backdrop of this incredible space.

The materials of the civil engineering structure form a rugged backdrop for the hierarchy of finished elements such as escalators and acoustically absorptive surfaces. The structure is constructed in concrete that has been lightly sand blasted, exposing the mica in the concrete mix and giving a sparkling reflective quality to the finished surface. The escalators are clad in highly finished perforated panels to improve acoustics and the

clarity of the public address system. Lighting is achieved by a combination of indirect sources, illuminating both the structural form and materials, and the passenger routes for safety purposes. Services are distributed in a combination of concealed and exposed accessible systems to accommodate future technological developments. Access for the disabled is provided by lifts serving all platform levels.

Construction work took six years to complete at a cost of around £20 million. Throughout this period the District and Circle Line remained open and fully operational.

ticket hall roof concrete diagrid

the escalator 'box'

section: east west

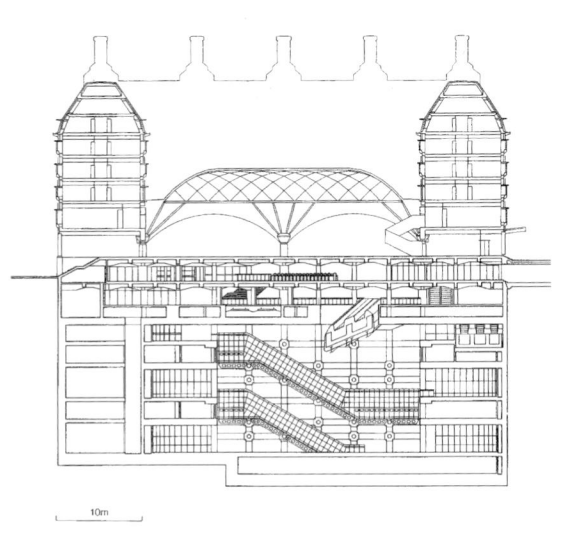

10m

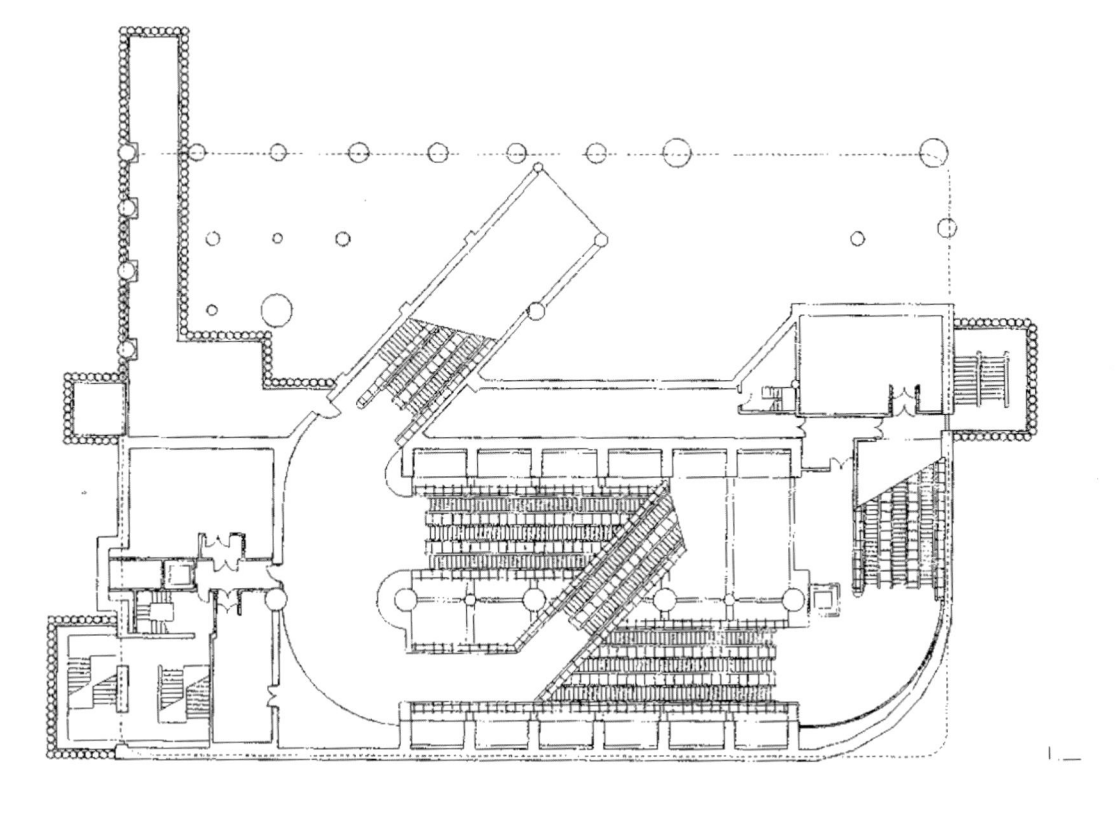

plan: intermediate level

The eastbound tunnel would run directly above the westbound tunnel to minimise disturbance of Big Ben's foundations.

Discussion with John Pringle, formerly project partner of Michael Hopkins, responsible for the design of Westminster Station

JLE appointed us in order to achieve a single architect designing Westminster Station and the new Parliamentary building above. At an early stage the engineers, Maunsell, wrote an outstanding paper on the engineering problems and how best to minimise the disturbance to the existing building and tunnels under Bridge Street. In summary, all tunnels would be bored with the smallest possible diameter to reduce the volume of excavation; the eastbound tunnel would run

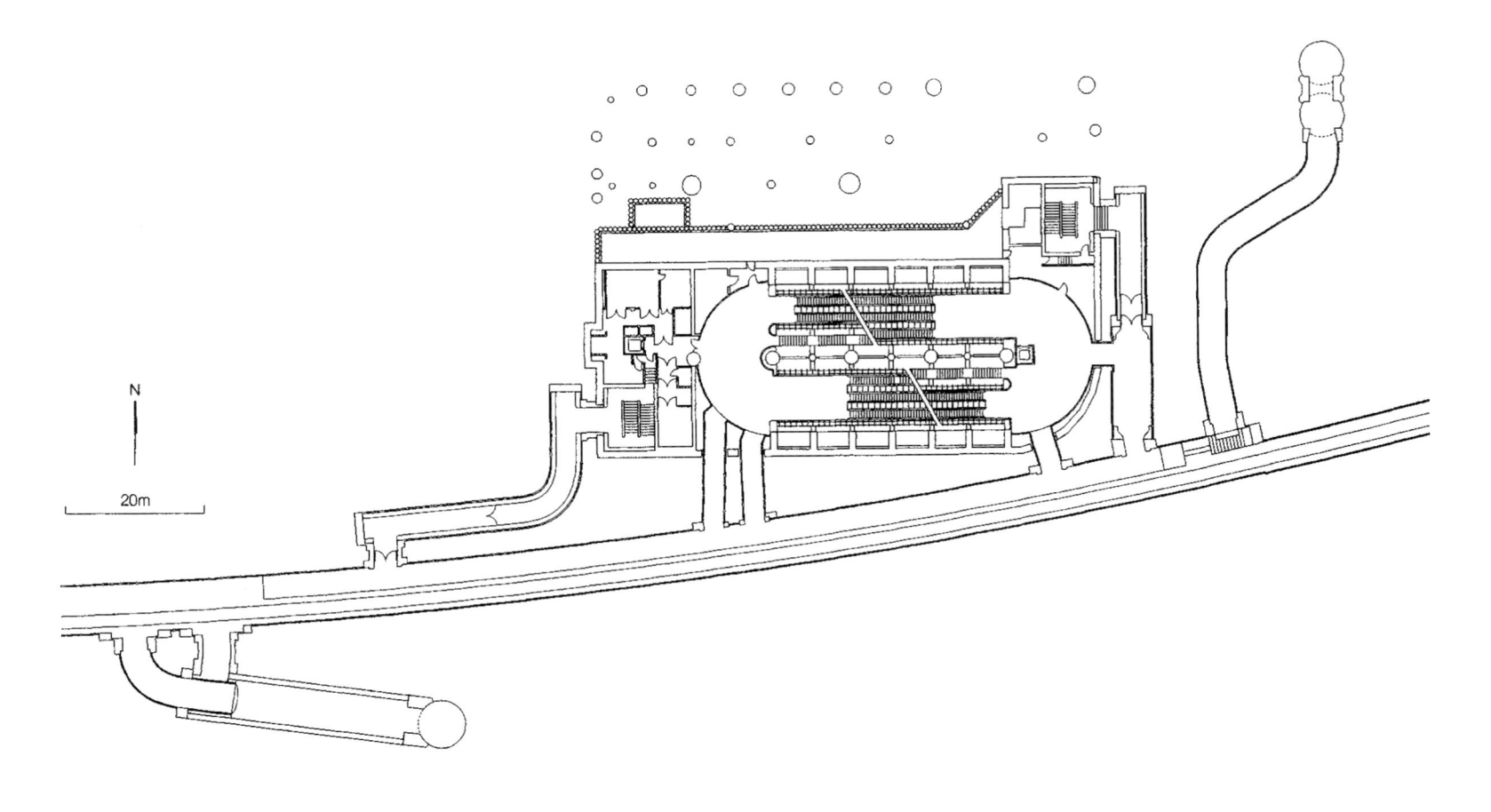

**plan: jubilee line level
eastbound**

To retain the diaphragm walls, a grillage of heavy beams and columns was cast against it to receive the muscular steel cross bracing. The visibility of the entire construction expresses the giant forces that are acting on the wall and structural supports.

directly above the westbound tunnel to minimise disturbance of Big Ben's foundations, and the station box would be constructed using diaphragm walling techniques. The width of the deep shaft of the station box would allow six 2 m diameter laterally braced mega-columns (supporting the transfer slab of Portcullis House), to run through it onto piled foundations. As architects we saw a fantastic opportunity to show off the civil engineering of the whole structure.

As the excavation progressed, the engineering solution of bracing the diaphragm walls using the floor slabs was going to make the shaft a dark and stuffy place. We reasoned with our engineers to keep the deep shaft an

open space by incorporating the temporary steel bracing tubes and flying shores as part of the permanent structure. Our argument was that if you create a seven-storey basement structure within a 30 m deep excavation, you have large areas of flooring and lighting to keep clean and maintain. By eliminating the solid floor slabs and replacing them with tubular cross bracing and shallow landings big enough to access the platform and escalators, we dramatically reduced the long-term costs for maintenance.

We were excited with the large cavernous space this created, with escalators climbing up to the surface. It was an underground cathedral, with the diaphragm walls left uncovered and rough with the imprint of London's

geology, telegraphing a million years of change. Ideas like this were inspired by the architect Michelucci in Florence who was interested in the earth's construction and in expressing its geology in the building of modern churches. We also thought about the stunning village settlements and churches dug out of the rock face in Petra and Cappadocia.

To retain the diaphragm walls, a grillage of heavy beams and columns was cast against it to receive the muscular steel cross bracing. The visibility of the entire construction expresses the giant forces that are acting on the wall and structural supports. We coated the tubular steel bracing members with rust-inhibiting

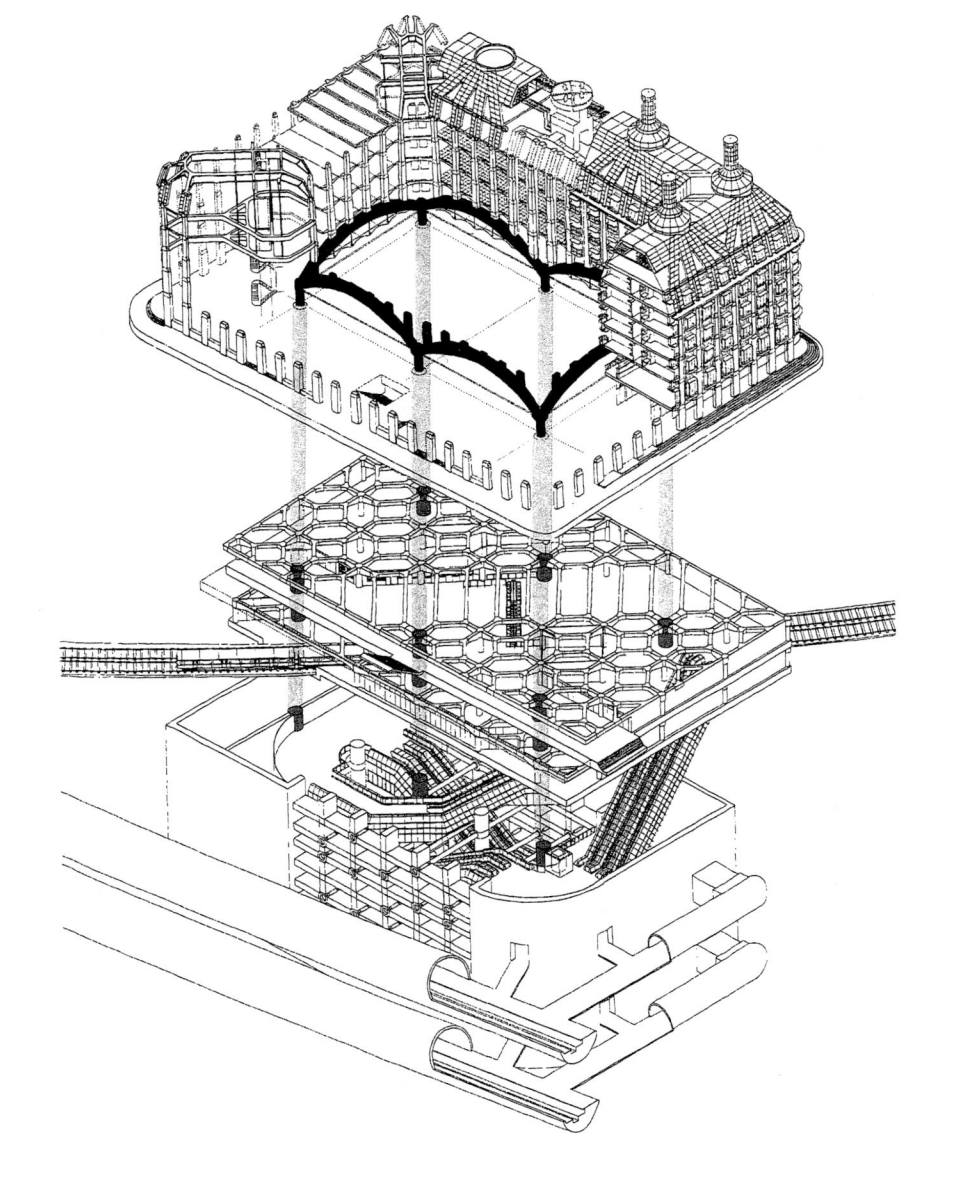

paintwork and left the vertical concrete grillage with a natural concrete finish to let the power and honesty of the engineering become the architectural statement.

The grillage of beams and columns against the walls casts dark and light shadows that accentuate the drama of the whole space. We continued the vocabulary of the flying shores and beam grillage upwards, repeating it for the 'diagrid' ceiling of the ticket hall roof slab. The columns in the ticket hall were designed with a taper, the beams' depths were reduced at mid-span with a haunch at the column, to ensure that there was adequate headroom. The concrete roof was cast with a natural exposed finish.

The concrete in the ticket hall and those areas close to public view was wet sand blasted to give a fine, uniform appearance. The wet blast was light and the size of grit was determined after we had carried out trials. For the formed finishes we were quite happy to show off the nail heads and panel joints and bolt holes. Where the grillage beams holding back the diaphragm wall come close to the escalators in the ticket hall, the surface has been bush hammered.

What was achieved was far better than sticking on tiles or overcladding the concrete. Anti-graffiti coating was sprayed on all the concrete surfaces that would come into contact with people. The finish to the platform

section has been left as the cast-iron rings of tunnel lining, inter-clad with stove-enamelled panels copied from the ones at London Bridge. We used George Sexton as our lighting consultant.

We were given a lot of freedom to design the station and working with our civil engineering partner, Maunsell, was ultimately rewarding. We had little contact with the tunnelling engineers as they were a law unto themselves, nor any direct contact with the contractor, even though we carried out the detailed design work of the station.

Civil Engineer: Maunsell
Contractor: Balfour Beatty–AMEC

two

© **Southwark** Architect: MacCormac Jamieson Prichard

Richard MacCormac, MacCormac Jamieson Prichard

The brief that was given by the client defined the physical constraints of the site, the alignment and depth of the tunnels and the projected number of people the station would have to accommodate. There were drawings indicating the service cables, sewers, gas, electricity and water mains buried in the pavement or across the site. The architect was required to work out a plan of how to get from the surface entrances to the platform levels in the most efficient and logical way.

The main objective of the design, therefore, was to maximise passenger comfort and security by minimising the complexity of the station. This was achieved by distinguishing and enhancing the volumetric characteristics of the passenger areas.

preliminary sketch of
lower concourse
(platform level)

The main objective of the design, therefore, was to maximise passenger comfort and security by minimising the complexity of the station. This was achieved by distinguishing and enhancing the volumetric characteristics of the passenger areas. Architecturally it is intended to be an easily understood and enjoyable place to begin and end a journey.

The station is constructed as a large cut-and-cover box that is 16 m deep, 40 m long and which is enclosed by a roof that rises 4 m above ground level and is visible from Blackfriars Road. In order to bring as much daylight as possible into the concourse, a series of tilting mirrors were proposed which would be fixed to the railway viaduct that ran on the western boundary of the site. The mirrors would bounce sunlight into the concourse and reflect it down into the lower concourse and the

train tunnels. Frederick Wagner worked as the consultant on this concept for nearly a year, before it was abandoned because the escalators had to be accommodated in three small diameter tunnels, instead of two larger ones.

The intermediate concourse of the station is a transition between the entrances at ground level on Blackfriars Road and Waterloo East, and the platforms below ground. Southwark provides a much more convenient connection to Waterloo East railway station, which is connected to Waterloo mainline as well as the Northern and Bakerloo Lines through the terminus. This pedestrian confluence, where the two pedestrian flows meet before continuing down to platform level, had to be a large space that would disengage the flow of pedestrians from the tunnels as they connected to the platforms.

cone wall and roof
beam

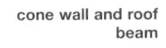

axonometric: access
ground to platform
level

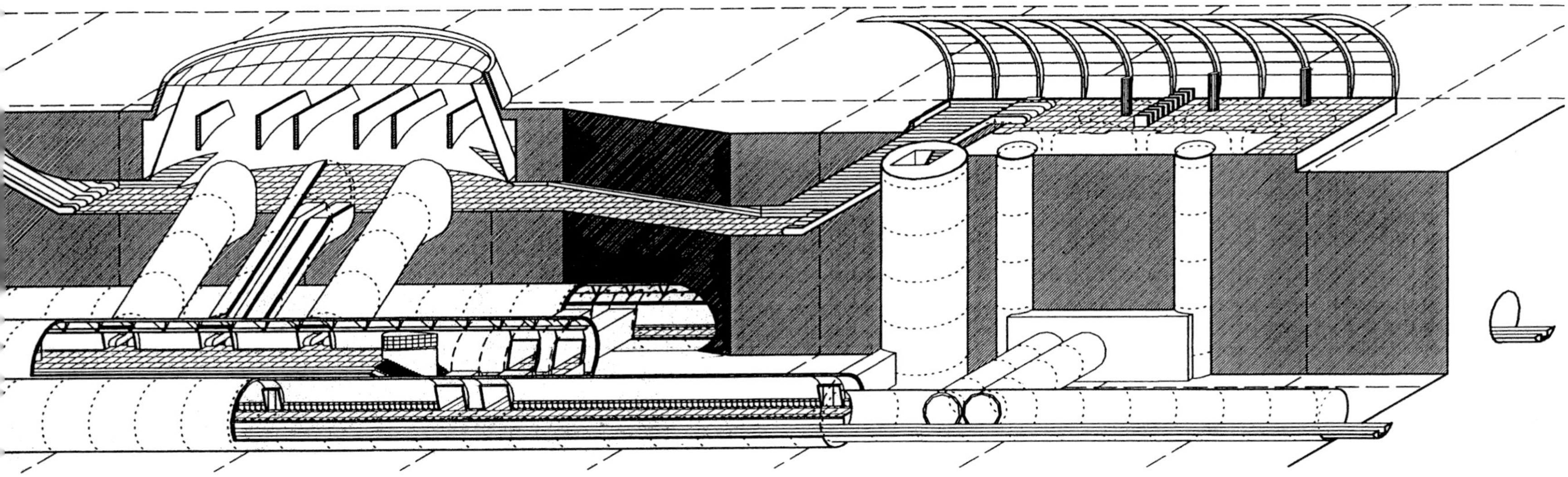

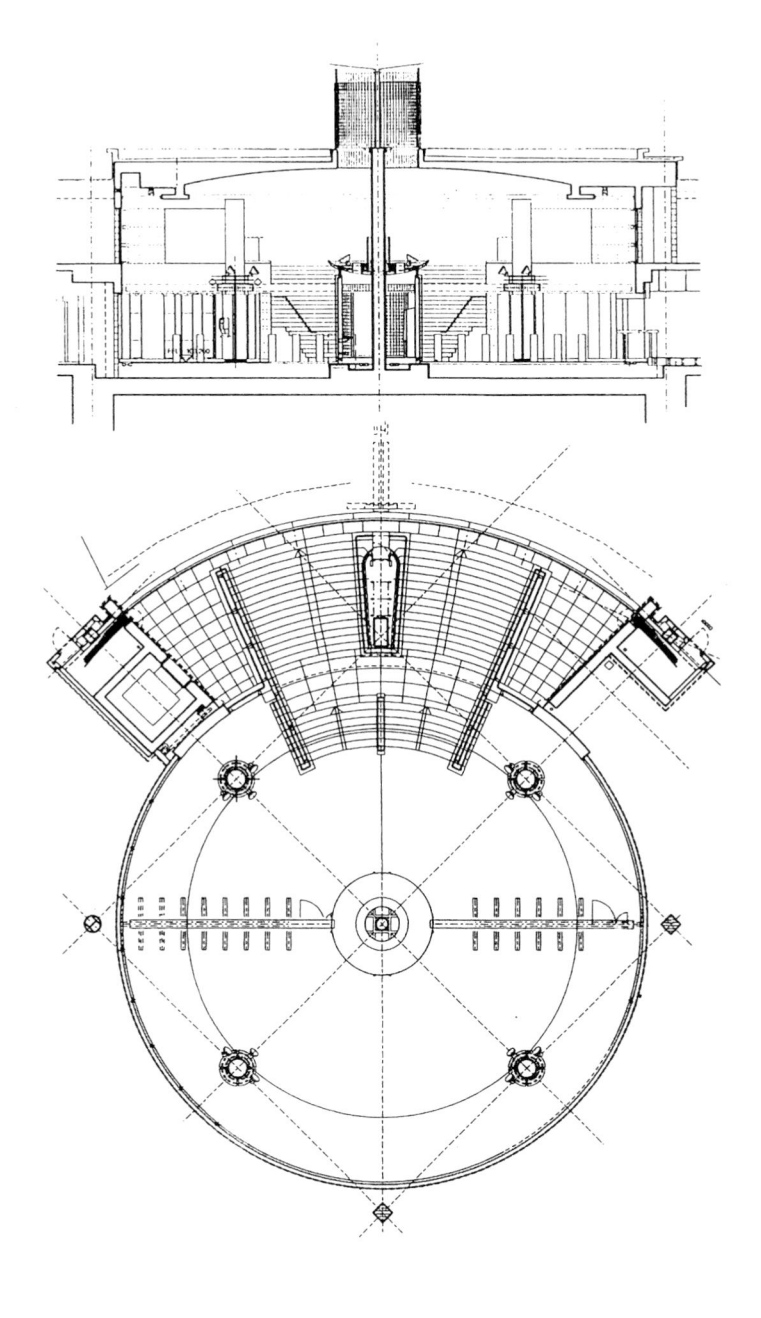

Originally the curved wall was drawn as an arc of a circle and was to be cast in polished white concrete. Later the geometry changed to become a cone so as to avoid blocking the escalator engine access covers, just behind the curved wall.

The walls of the intermediate concourse are quite contrasting. One wall is deliberately straight in plan and faced with polished concrete blockwork and the other is curved and clad in blue tinted glass. The polished blockwork wall contains the arched entrances to the escalator tunnels that descend to the platforms. The entrances to the escalator tunnels have a pronounced lip because of the wall's raking repose. If you look up the escalator you will see that the cylindrical enclosure continues to the top in an unbroken line. The reason for maintaining the rake of the escalator shaft was to

maximise the view of the cone wall and to avoid the opening looking like a tiny mouse hole.

For the other flank wall we decided to mask the civil engineering structure with a curved facade. The curvature was necessary to define more clearly the travel route to and from the ticket hall and the escalators within the box. The curving wall, or cone wall, signals the change of direction for pedestrian traffic flow and defines the space within the concourse coherently so that people travel with purpose rather than turn arbitrarily looking for signage.

White concrete blade beams strut the top of the box near the roof. To minimise obstruction to daylight, the profile of the beams was deliberately tapered to make them appear as deep slender blades rather than chunky logs. Originally the curved wall was drawn as an arc of a circle and was to be cast in polished white concrete. Later the geometry changed to become a cone so as to avoid blocking the escalator engine access covers, just behind the curved wall. The internal wall was pushed outwards to form a conical section, which had an elliptical curvature. The problem now was how to clad a conical surface with an

ticket hall

elliptical plan geometry. After some brainstorming the idea of using triangular glass tiles emerged. Working with Hanif Kara of YRM, Anthony Hunt and artist Alex Beleschenko, the architect used a computer model to refine a pattern of 1200 mm high triangular tiles that would fit the geometry of the cone wall.

Beleschenko devised an enamel fritting to the tiles to graduate their opacity as they run from the base of the concourse to the roof. From the base of the wall up to eye level the tiles are a translucent blue, which gets

progressively lighter in colour towards the top. Four different fritting patterns were generated for the 630 tiles. The glass tiles are held in place at their corners by a stainless steel spider, which connects to the steel frame support structure. The spider connections were designed to withstand the wind load generated by the drafts of air that are pushed out by the trains as they emerge from the tunnels.

The lower concourse, that leads directly to the platforms on either side, occupies a 9 m diameter tunnel. There are

two levels to the concourse, the higher level, which runs in the middle section of the concourse and receives the three escalator banks from the intermediate concourse, and the lower levels on either end, which lead to the platforms. The concourse is lined with stainless steel panels on a modular plan dictated by the sectional grids of the actual tunnel segments. Overhead lighting and up-lighters, some tinted pale blue, continue to reflect the blue of the cone wall on the stainless steel panels. Two 'heroic' curved pylons, rather like streamlined funnels, divide the staircases on either end of the high-level walkway. The

lower concourse, platform level

staircase and funnel of
light

Overhead lighting and up-lighters, some tinted pale blue, continue to reflect the blue of the cone wall on the stainless steel panels. Two 'heroic' curved pylons, rather like streamlined funnels, divide the staircases on either end of the high-level walkway.

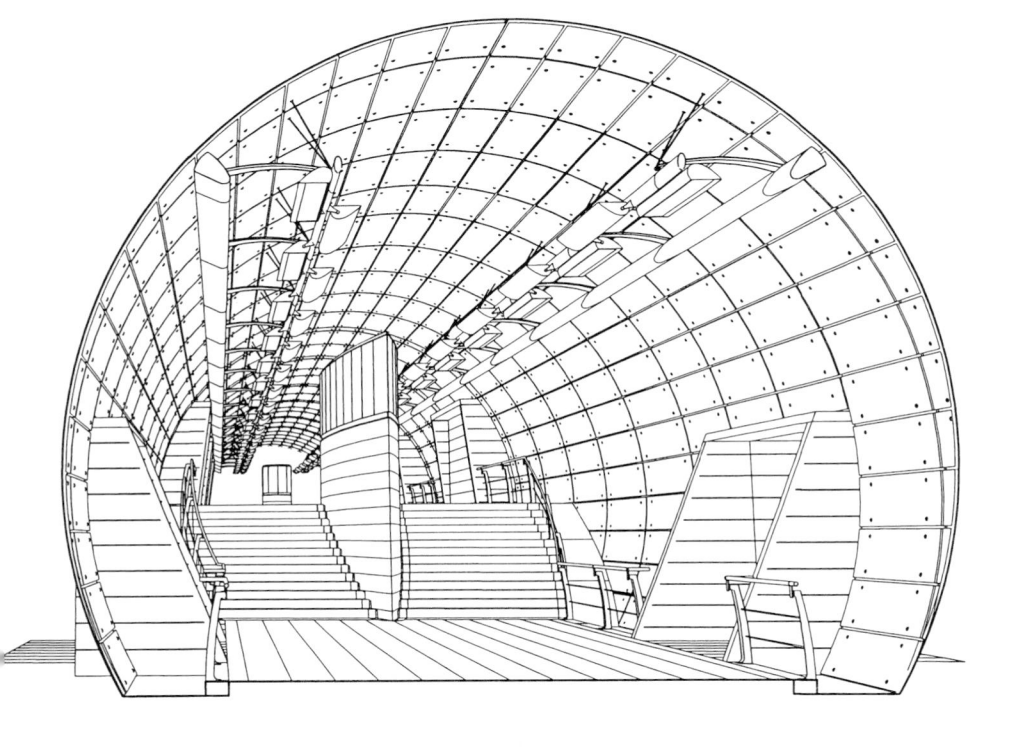

schematic: lower
concourse

top half of the pylons are illuminated, the intention was to make them appear as beacons that telegraph the position of the staircase and direct people towards the exit points. The platforms themselves continue the theme of tough, resilient materials but with an enhanced quality using textured masonry and enamelled glass. A continuous solid 'resting' bench reinforces the normal seating along the platform, while an illuminated glass frieze 'names' the station.

To enhance the internal space of the lower concourse, the floor is disengaged architecturally from the tunnels by illuminating the floor from below. The adits leading to the platforms have been interpreted as bridges, with an attempt to create a visual landscape with blue up-lighters to simulate sky and white light boxes that pick

Waterloo East:
entrance and canopy

The design intent was to create a topographical architecture – a subterranean landscape consisting of alternating experiences of confinement and spatial expansion, each amplified by the intervention of natural and artificial light.

up the edges of the staircase and floors, creating an architecture where signage was unnecessary. The entrance and exit points and the access spaces could be clearly read in the building form.

The Blackfriars Road ticket hall draws on the designs of the Holden stations of the 1930s. It is enclosed in a large double drum, 20 m in diameter, with a gently domed ceiling. The primary structure of the hall is high-quality white concrete and stainless steel. The higher concrete canopy forms a portico above which will ultimately sit a fifteen-storey housing development. The lower canopy in steel and glass illuminates and heralds the entrance to the station.

In all the deliberations with their civil engineering team, the architects led the design discussions on the size,

shape and plan of the stations. The engineers acted as benevolent policemen, reacting and responding to architectural suggestions, always looking for the simple, least risky solution.

The architectural principal followed throughout the structure was to respect and respond to the civil engineering envelope, which was developed with the engineers. The design intent was to create a topographical architecture – a subterranean landscape consisting of alternating experiences of confinement and spatial expansion, each amplified by the intervention of natural and artificial light.

Civil Engineer: Babtie–DHV
Contractor: Aoki–Soletanche

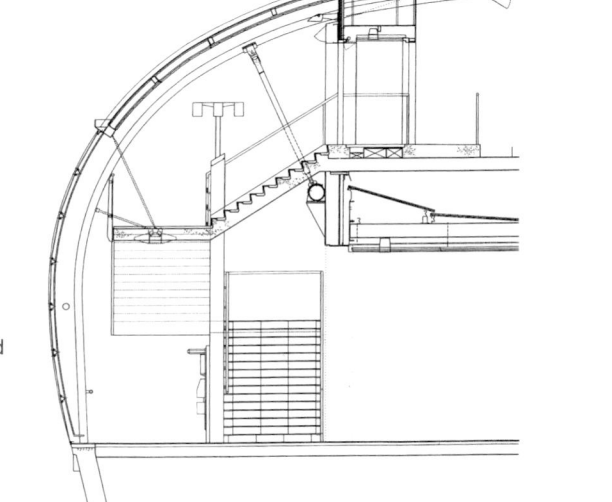

schematic:
intermediate concourse
and cone wall

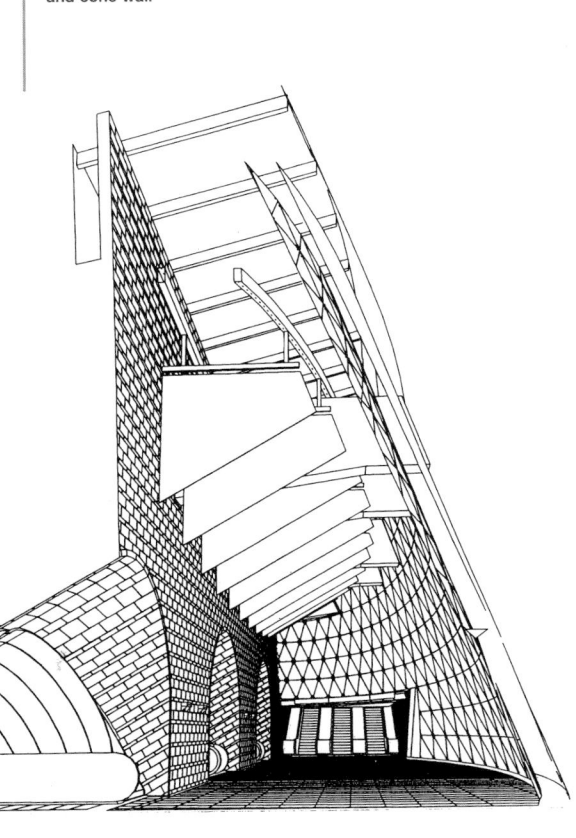

intermediate concourse

↙ **Jubilee line**

↙ **Jubilee line**

↑ Way out   Blackfriars Road   Tate Mo

three

 **Waterloo** Architect: JLE Project Architects

Simon Moore, Nicholas Grimshaw Architects (formerly of JLE Project Architects)

Notwithstanding its modest appearance, Waterloo Station is not only a highly efficient piece of station design, it is also a paradox. The fragility of the old mainline stations above the new underground tunnels compelled London Underground to insist on the use of traditional cast-iron tunnel construction and ensure the diameter did not exceed 10 m, as a precaution against large settlements and ground movements.

ticket hall: glass screen wall

axonometric plan

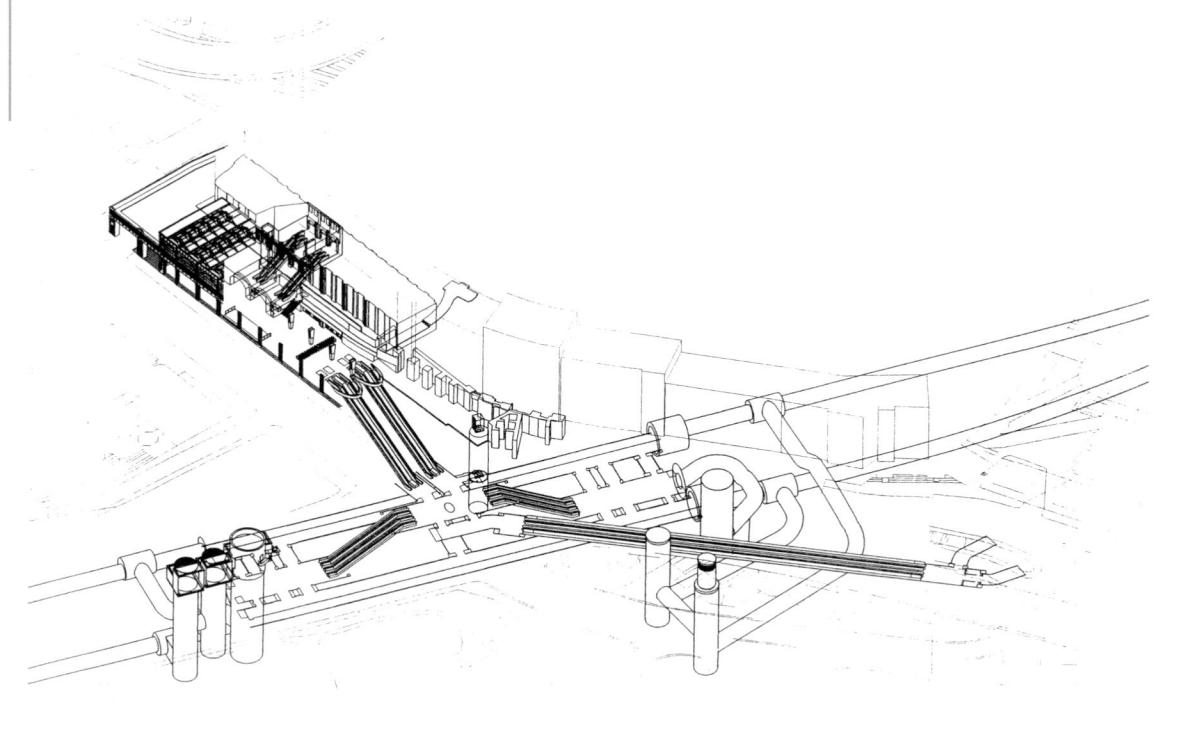

A glass screen encloses the colonnade and public areas for ticket purchase, while maintaining the visual link between the colonnade and the street.

Cast-iron, the most proven and secure of all tunnelling methods, was historically the material of the tube and responsible for its longevity. Normally it is lined and hidden from view as it can leak at the joints, but the Hong Kong MTR experience did show us that if properly grouted and caulked, it could be made leak-free. This gave us the confidence to make a feature of the material.

Our original plan was to locate the JLE ticket hall below the mainline station concourse. Although the space was generous, it would have to be artificially lit and connected to street level by a passageway. There was the added difficulty that the tunnelling and excavation work must not disrupt the rail services above it. The designs for the layout were well advanced when one of our team suggested that the colonnade on Waterloo Road – which was originally being used for goods deliveries and as a pull-in for buses – would be a better location for the ticket hall as it removed many of the constraints of the original location. After detailed engineering investigation this suggestion proved feasible and made generous economic savings. The colonnade now forms the ticket hall, with natural light and artificial up-lighting flooding the area to reveal the original Edwardian brickwork and girders that have been restored.

The ticket hall design can be viewed as a series of modern insertions into the fabric of the old station structure. The central space is the Edwardian colonnade which has been widened by the removal of four brick vaults. An angled, buttressed concrete wall replaces the brick vaults, and acts as a retaining structure housing the ticket office. The concrete ticket hall structure has exposed concrete waffle slab soffits, the modern

The designs for the layout were well advanced when one of our team suggested that the colonnade on Waterloo Road – which was originally being used for goods deliveries and as a pull-in for buses – would be a better location for the ticket hall as it removed many of the constraints of the original location.

pier and intercom

equivalent of the brick 'jack arches' in the Edwardian colonnade. A glass screen encloses the colonnade and public areas for ticket purchase, while maintaining the visual link between the colonnade and the street. The glass panels of the screen are supported on twin posts, which are held at the top by horizontal stainless steel rods fixed to the existing 'jack arches'. These stainless steel rods hold the top of the posts in a sleeving device that allows for vertical movement of the jack arches, which deflect quite significantly from the traffic loads that the colonnade supports. The ticket hall is naturally orientated towards the four large brick vaults, and contains escalators that lead to the underground tunnels. In front of the first two brick vaults we designed two elliptical openings through the ticket hall floor slab to take the escalators that descend to the platforms. A third arch leads to a spacious passageway and a steel-clad free-standing lift that descends to platform level.

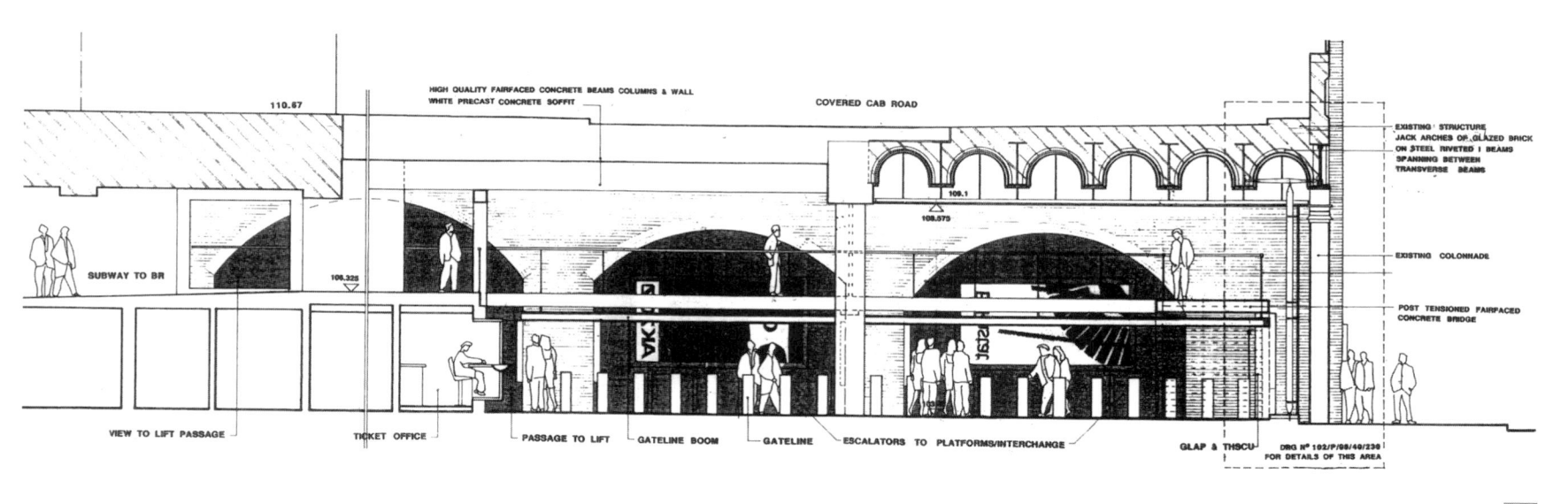

Waterloo Road entrance

110.67

HIGH QUALITY FAIRFACED CONCRETE BEAMS COLUMNS & WALL
WHITE PRECAST CONCRETE SOFFIT

COVERED CAB ROAD

EXISTING STRUCTURE
JACK ARCHES OF GLAZED BRICK
ON STEEL RIVETED I BEAMS
SPANNING BETWEEN
TRANSVERSE BEAMS

109.1
108.575

108.325

SUBWAY TO BR

EXISTING COLONNADE

POST TENSIONED FAIRFACED
CONCRETE BRIDGE

VIEW TO LIFT PASSAGE   TICKET OFFICE   PASSAGE TO LIFT   GATELINE BOOM   GATELINE   ESCALATORS TO PLATFORMS/INTERCHANGE   GLAP & THSCU

DRG N° 102/P/08/40/230
FOR DETAILS OF THIS AREA

upper concourse and glass walled stair pod

lighting boom fixing
assembly

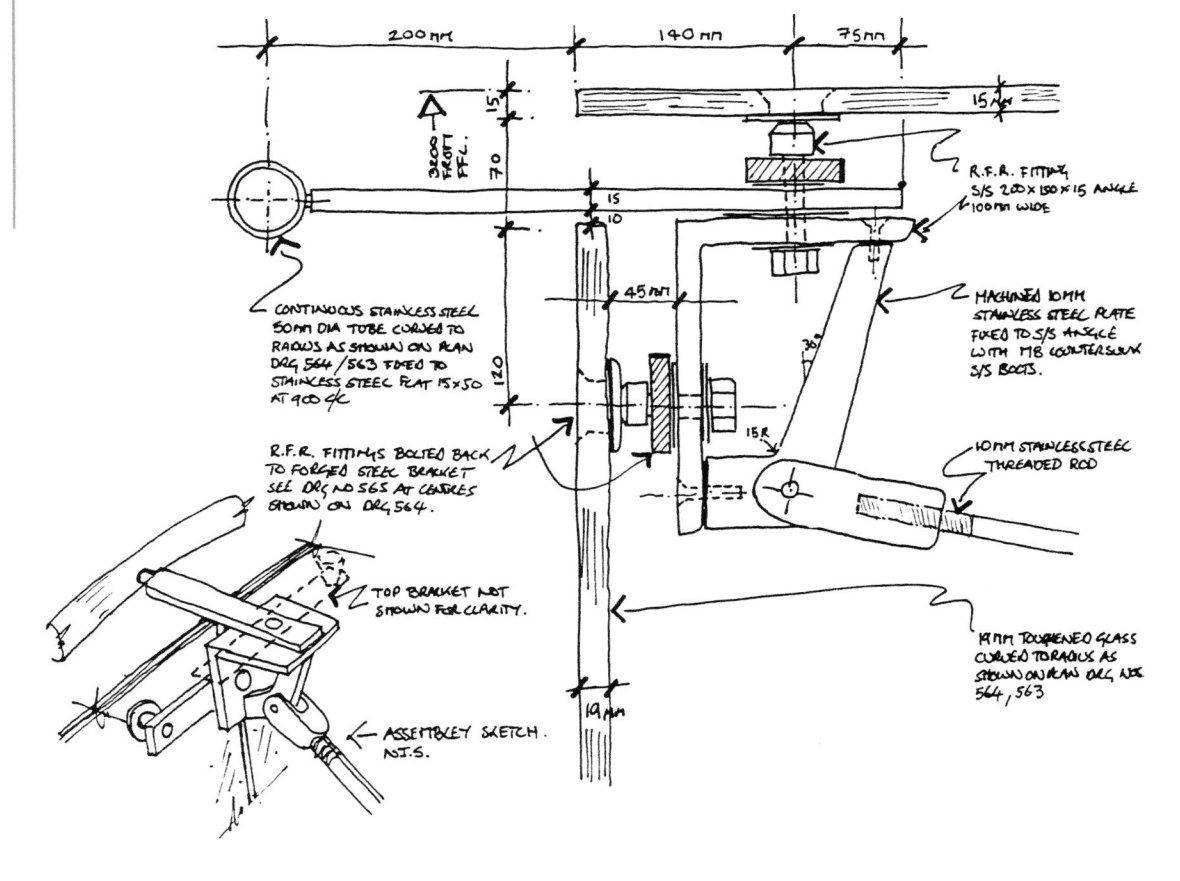

200 mm   140 mm   75 mm

3200 FROM FFL.

R.F.R. FITTING
S/S 200 x 150 x 15 ANGLE
100 mm WIDE

CONTINUOUS STAINLESS STEEL
50 mm DIA TUBE CURVED TO
RADIUS AS SHOWN ON PLAN
DRG 564 / 563 FIXED TO
STAINLESS STEEL FLAT 15 x 50
AT 900 c/c

MACHINED 10 mm
STAINLESS STEEL PLATE
FIXED TO S/S ANGLE
WITH M8 COUNTERSUNK
S/S BOLTS.

R.F.R. FITTINGS BOLTED BACK
TO FORGED STEEL BRACKET
SEE DRG NO 565 AT CENTRES
SHOWN ON DRG 564.

10 mm STAINLESS STEEL
THREADED ROD

TOP BRACKET NOT
SHOWN FOR CLARITY.

19 mm TOUGHENED GLASS
CURVED TO RADIUS AS
SHOWN ON PLAN DRG NOS
564, 563

ASSEMBLY SKETCH.
N.T.S.

This approach can also be seen in the upper concourse tunnel where the stairs leading to the escalator machine room are enclosed by an elliptical glass enclosure.

Though it is one of the deepest stations of the line, passengers are taken from the ticket hall to platforms through measured spaces that are easy to follow. The ticket hall is naturally orientated towards the arched vaults. Directly under two of these vaults are the banks of escalators that thread their way down to an intermediate concourse, where there is a 140 m long travelator to provide a link to the Northern and Bakerloo Lines. To the left and right of the travelator, two further sets of escalators drop down to serve two lower concourses. We worked hard to find an effective junction detail that allowed the tubular escalator tunnels to rise and meet the ticket hall floor and cut through the

brick-walled viaduct. By positioning the escalator junctions away from the walls, and surrounding the oval escalator openings through the ticket hall floor with a polished steel handrail and fascia, the entry point for the escalators was neatly resolved. This approach can also be seen in the upper concourse tunnel where the stairs leading to the escalator machine room are enclosed by an elliptical glass enclosure.

The upper concourse is the hub of the station and it is where the true engineering feat of Waterloo takes place. Six large cast-iron tunnels come together at one place only 8 m below the old Victorian railway viaduct.

Settlement was a real problem and extensive measures were taken to overcome this, including a highly refined system of compensation grouting.

As the tunnels and the construction was the means of expression for the architecture of the stations, our collaboration with the engineers went beyond the layout design of the whole station. It included the detailed design of key junctions, and the detailing of the cast-iron and other linings that form the tunnels and concourses. By having such design input on the panel layouts (the position of bolt holes and grout holes, the type of finish and colour of the segments) we were able to enhance the overall

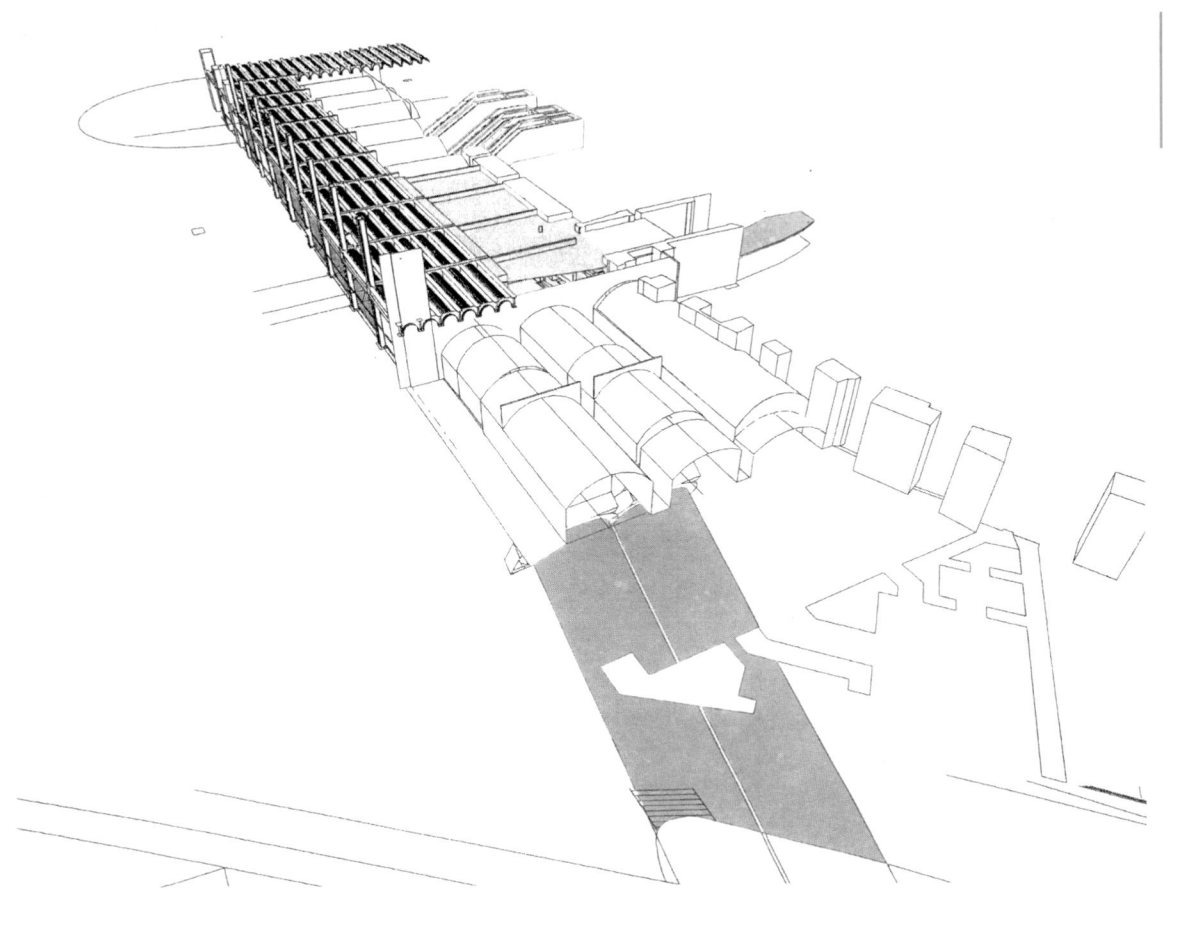

appearance of them so that they were not only the structure but also part of the finished system. The problem of locating electrical services, normally seen bundled and tacked to the walls of the existing tube system, plus the plethora of signs and bits of station equipment, were also explored, rationalised and neatly contained.

At platform level the NATM (New Austrian Tunnelling Method) was used instead of cast-iron tunnel linings. This enabled us to create recesses to house the bulkiest platform components making these platforms particularly free of clutter. Grey mosaic tiles were fixed directly to the in situ concrete walls, to maintain the tunnel form appearance.

We worked with the diverse disciplines of tunnel contractors, track alignment specialists, ventilation engineers, passenger movement planners and our civil engineer counterparts. We often questioned the way things were being done and could be done, driven by our motivation to reveal more of the construction of the tunnelled structure. To their credit the engineers accepted the challenge and with our encouragement pushed the system to the limit to achieve the directness and clarity of the architecture we were seeking.

Civil Engineer: Maunsell
Contractor: Balfour Beatty–Amec

escalator opening and handrail

The ticket hall design can be viewed as a series of modern insertions into the fabric of the old station structure. The central space is the Edwardian colonnade which has been widened by the removal of four brick vaults.

entrance: glass wall
and roof canopy

main entrance

commencing with the scale, mass and surface
irregularity of the diaphragm walls; the sharp horizontal
form of the deep concrete trusses; and the monolithic
qualities of the vertical 'blade' walls, with secondary
finishes reduced to the absolute minimum.

The treatment of the above-ground structure and
internal fit out of the public areas continues this
construction hierarchy by expressing the metal castings,

stainless steel plate, blue glass frieze and glass seats.
The quality of the concrete finish has been carefully
reviewed to achieve a balance between economy,
practicality and quality. A ground, granulated, blast-
furnace slag cement ('ggbs' for short) was selected to
improve the appearance of all exposed concrete. It
produces a warm, pale grey concrete. The blade walls to
the escalator void incorporate a particular sand-
aggregate matrix designed to enhance the surface

finish, with a lightness of colour tone and light
reflectance.

At street level the station roof emerges from below
ground with a gentle curve, rising towards Jamaica
Road. The roof cantilevers over the main entrance and
public footway to form a protective canopy. It is a
glazed, translucent structure supported by slender
beams that are wrapped in perforated, stainless steel. It

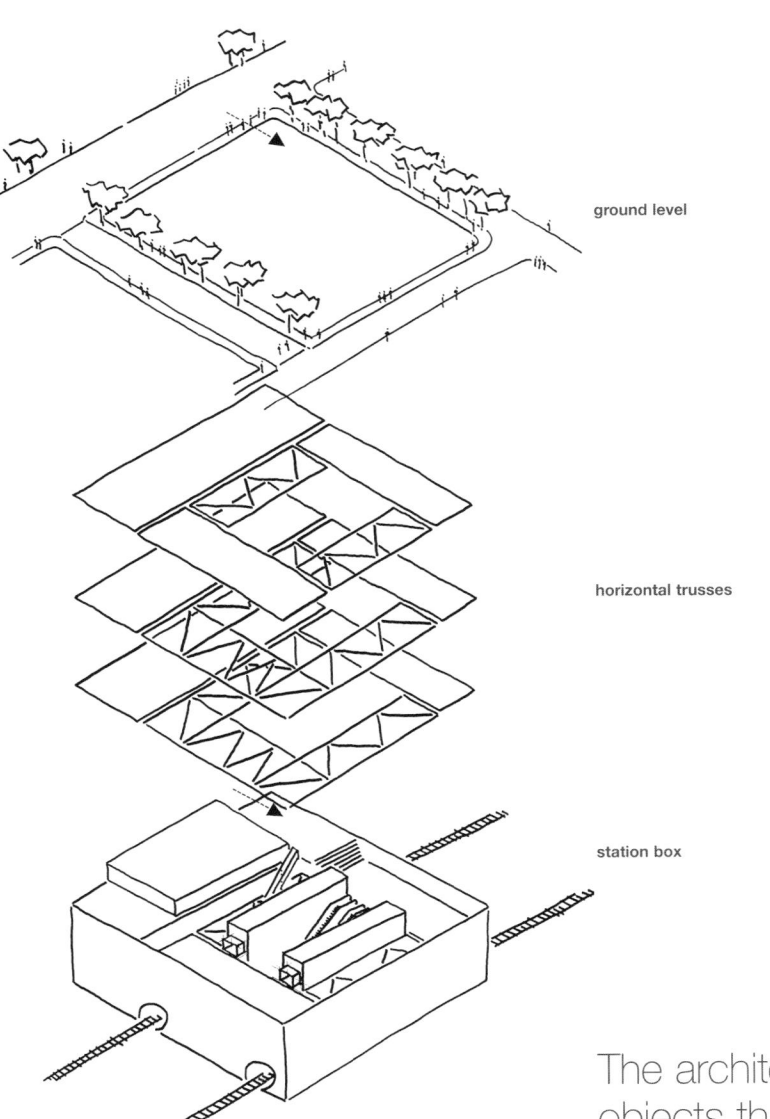

ground level

horizontal trusses

station box

The architectural intention was to create a family of sculptural objects that articulate the functional character of the shafts.

has been designed to take full advantage of daylight and sunlight within all public areas and the below-ground structure, alleviating the sense of tension and claustrophobia often associated with sub-surface environments. The support beams interfere with the play of natural light passing through the glazed panels, casting reflections and shadows onto the surrounding surfaces.

The perimeter of the building is clad in transparent glazing allowing visibility into the station and to the trains below. The design of the building seeks to reinforce the public entrance which fronts Jamaica Road, by introducing trees along both Major Road and Keetons Road. Artificial lighting in the station is arranged to enhance the visual quality of the public areas and to articulate the structure of the interior.

Durands Wharf Vent Shaft

The JLE has been designed with ventilation and intervention shafts at 1000 m intervals between stations. The design team has been responsible for six of these shafts between London Bridge and Canary Wharf Stations. The architectural intention was to create a family of sculptural objects that articulate the functional character of the shafts – the air movement, plant rooms, escape and access shafts. As the design of each shaft developed, the surface manifestations became increasingly more site specific, placing less emphasis on the 'family' connection and more on locally responsive expression. The principal forms chosen for the shafts were carved monoliths, vertical blade walls, curved horizontal planes or bands and filigree 'mesh' screens. These forms would be made from a palette of materials that include smooth creamy-concrete, polished black

concrete trusses

sketch: landscaping
and frontage on Major
Road

Jamaica Road frontage

The curved walls appear to emerge from the ground, slicing open the landscape, suggesting the larger structure buried below ground.

basalt aggregate concrete, stainless steel wire meshes, and metal plate of copper, galvanised steel and stainless steel. Planting and landscaping are also an essential ingredient of the design, providing a seasonally changing foil for the architecture of the structure. Lighting has been included for public safety and security and to dramatise the forms.

The Durands Wharf shaft responds to the narrow and elongated route of the tunnels running below ground and the height restriction on the surface, related to the landscape of Durands Wharf Park, in which it is sited.

Two intersecting curved concrete walls form an outer 'curtain wall' enclosing the plant and equipment courtyards, ventilation shaft and shaft access door. The curved walls appear to emerge from the ground, slicing open the landscape, suggesting the larger structure buried below ground. The air intake of the ventilation shaft takes the form of an inverted cone formed by a filigree cable mesh that is positioned between the two walls, and a double curved stainless steel roof.

The constituents of the concrete walls have been designed to produce a light creamy-grey background

with a matrix of black basalt aggregates. The surface of the concrete has been ground off to expose the black basalt aggregates. The effect of the grinding is to express a continuity with the gravel and sands through which the tunnels have been bored, as well as revealing the 'handmade' process of casting and compacting concrete.

Civil Engineer: Sir William Halcrow and Partners
Contractor: Aoki Soletanche Joint Venture and
                    O'Rourke Civil Engineering

five

© **London Bridge** Architect: Weston Williamson Architects

Chris Williamson, Weston Williamson Architects

We were shortlisted for London Bridge by Roland Paoletti because he wanted to find young practices with a reputation for good architecture to design some of the stations. We had designed an overground station for Bognor Regis and had entered a competition for the Venice Bus Station but nothing quite prepared us for the challenge of the JLE. To get some inspiration for our ideas we looked at Bilbao, Washington, Paris Metro and Prague underground stations – the latter was particularly impressive. The brief we were given for the station was to express the civil engineering of the structure so that the users would see the clarity of its construction. The station was all below ground and within a network of tunnels that linked with the rail terminus of London Bridge and the Northern Line.

section: lower
concourse and platform
tunnels

schematic: tunnel lining
and stove-enamelled
panels

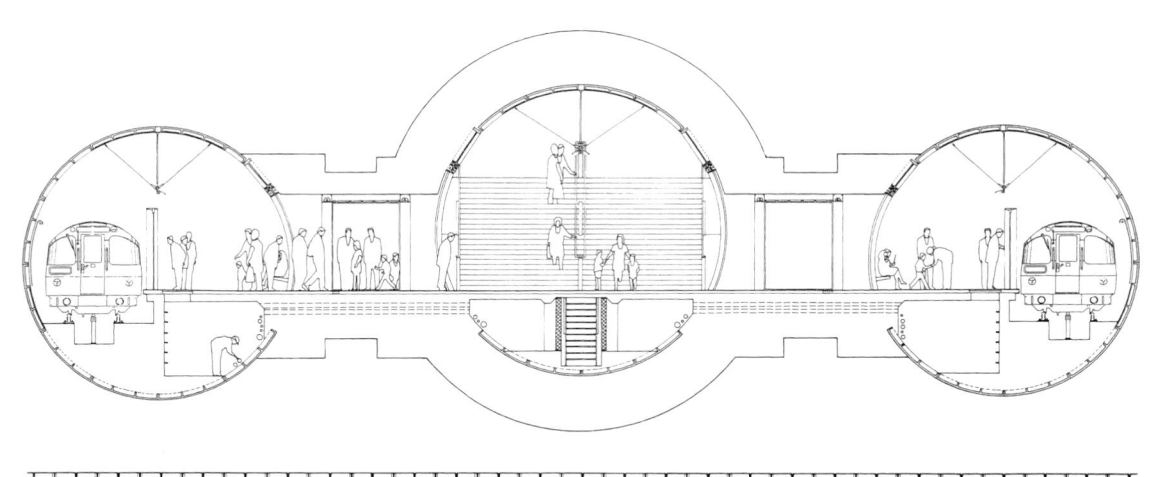

It was important to knit the
tunnels together to try to give
the whole station complex an
identity.

It was important to knit the tunnels together to try to give the whole station complex an identity. Cladding the bare structure over the areas where people could lean against it or touch the surface was considered. We wanted to cover places that could collect dirt and dust and eliminate as far as possible upstands, overhangs and ledges where grime could accumulate. The ceilings were designed with up-lighters to emphasise the height and breadth of the space. We wanted to treat the entrances and vent shafts as pieces of art and sculpture. The overhead lighting booms were positioned

to run continuously along the roof of the tunnels and interconnecting adit, into the mainline station. The lighting boom helps to focus the direction of travel, guiding you down to the platform and escalators. It was heartening to learn that the lighting was very much liked by the client.

The tunnel-lining segment had a boss onto which the stove-enamelled, cast-iron cover panels were connected. They had to be stove-enamelled to give the panel a 100-year life. The panels were cast by Glynwed

Foundries in Wales. They make cast-iron Aga cookers and have been doing so for around 70 years. The enamel can be chipped but it is extremely hardwearing and difficult to break off. We had some prototypes made and Mott MacDonald, our civil engineering partners – who were always supportive of our proposals – were keen to make them work. There was some concern expressed by the client regarding the safety and risk factor of such fittings, so the proposals had to be shown to their civil engineering counterparts in London Underground Ltd before they could approve it.

haunched concrete
roof beam

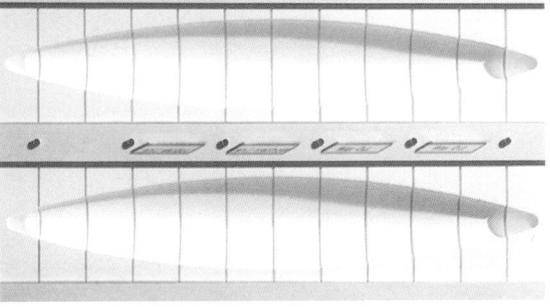

ceiling of lower concourse (platform level)

Jubilee line
← Westbound platform 3
Waterloo

Jubilee line
Eastbound platform 4 →
Stratford

The overhead lighting booms were positioned to run continuously along the roof of the tunnels and interconnecting adit, into the mainline station. The lighting boom helps to focus the direction of travel, guiding you down to the platform and escalators.

schematic: brick piers
and vaulted roof

concrete 'boots'
of brick piers

The cast-iron panels at the crown of the tunnel were slotted to reduce reverberation and sound reflection. Each panel measured 600 mm by 600 mm and cost £150, which works out at around £400/m^2 which was within the budget set for surface finishes. The benefit of cast-iron is that it will wear better than a tiled surface; it is not glued to a backing nor uses a secondary support system and is comparatively maintenance free.

We initially wanted the panels to be coloured either red, yellow or lime green – cheerfully bright and vibrant – but following discussion with the JLE Project Architects it was decided to make them blue so that if there was any severe vandalism the black subsurface would be less visible. For the Northern Line tunnels and adits, grey and white powder-coated cladding panels were specified that were not stove-enamelled cast-iron, to mark the distinction between the JLE and other transport corridors.

There was no contractual working relationship with Mott MacDonald as they were commissioned by the JLE Engineers and Weston Williamson were appointed by the JLE Project Architects. The civil engineers initially worked on the assumption that they would design a very utilitarian structure, bare and unfinished, and then hand it over to the architects to clad and decorate. They were surprised to find out at our first meeting that we were not working to the same brief. At one of the meetings we saw details of the cast-iron segments for the tunnel

aluminium seating pod

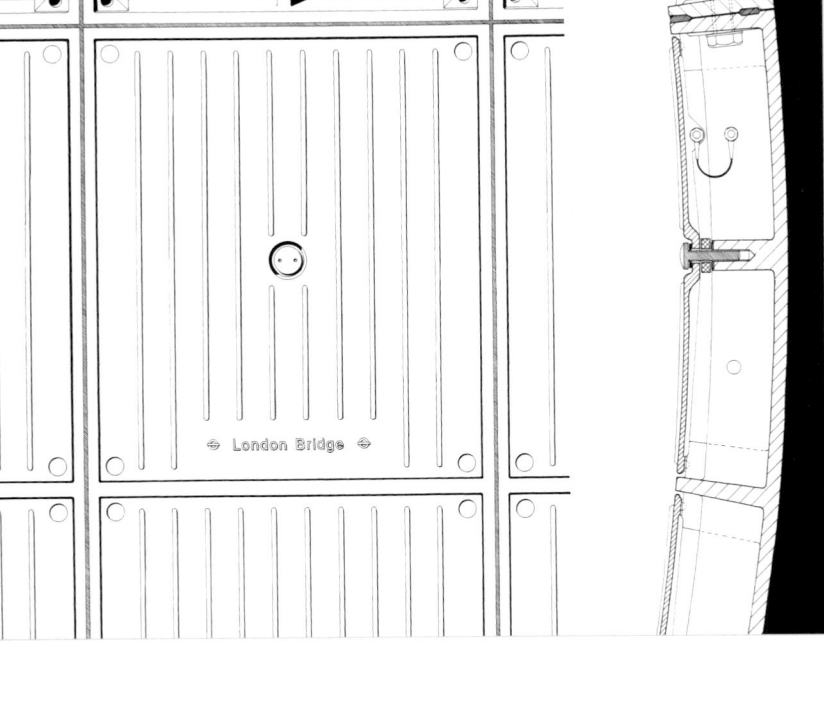

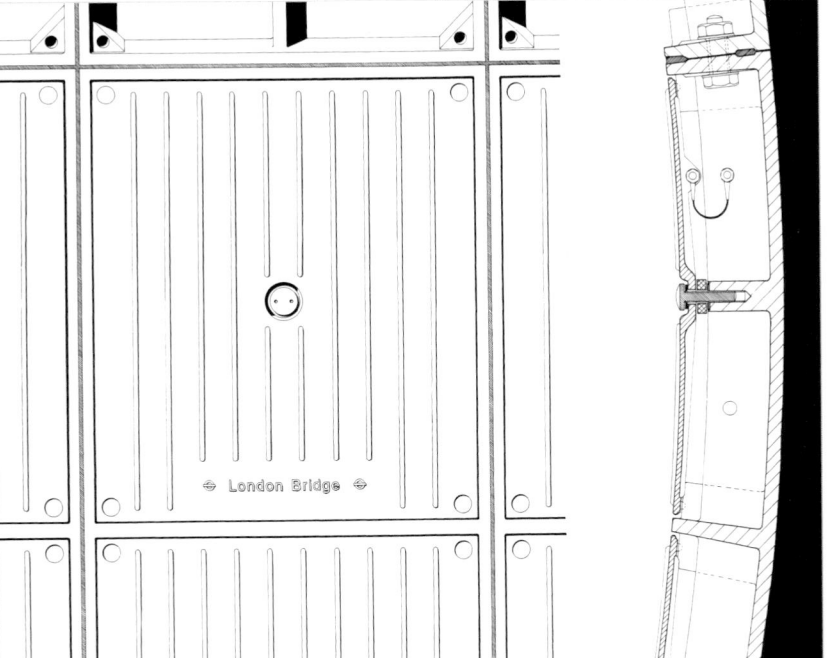

⊕ London Bridge ⊕

detail: stove-enamelled panel and cast-iron lining

lighting boom

NOTE UPLIGHTERS TO BE LOCATED IN ADITS AND ESCALATORS IF HEAD HEIGHT IS SUFFICIENT.

NEXO OR SIMILAR UPLIGHT

FLEXIBLE CONDUIT

CAST ALUMINIUM BRACKET

(1)→

OR

↓

(2) UPLIGHT RECESSED INTO GAP

BAFFLES IN UPLIGHT TO PREVENT GLARE WHEN VIEWED FROM ABOVE

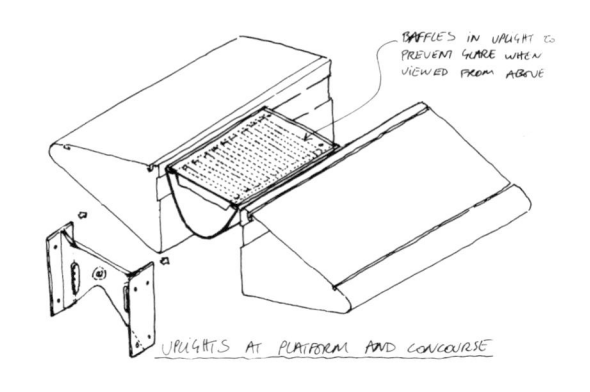

UPLIGHTS AT PLATFORM AND CONCOURSE

The tunnel-lining segment had a boss onto which the stove-enamelled, cast-iron cover panels were connected. They had to be stove-enamelled to give the panel a 100-year life.

lining and immediately hit upon the idea of expressing them in the architecture.

Our partnership with Mott MacDonald worked well, because we were interested in each others ideas and enjoyed the challenge of creating something a little more innovative and different. In planning the layout of the active tunnels, we introduced a rhythm and architectural hierarchy in expressing the structure – the headings over the openings, the proportion of covered panels to uncovered panels in the tunnel segments, the safety rail, the lighting strip along the platform, etc. We wanted to create a visual identity for London Bridge, so that

wherever you are within the underground network you will recognise the JLE station without the need for signage. On the Borough High Street entrance, as you come out of the escalator from the Northern Line, the ceiling has been expressed as a series of light-grey, haunched beams with a clear span of 12 m from wall to wall. The soffit of the plate girder beams are enclosed by a series of profiled precast segments, which reduce in depth towards the crown and provide the fire resistance and sound damping.

There are one or two aspects of the project that were not built as originally designed. For example changes were

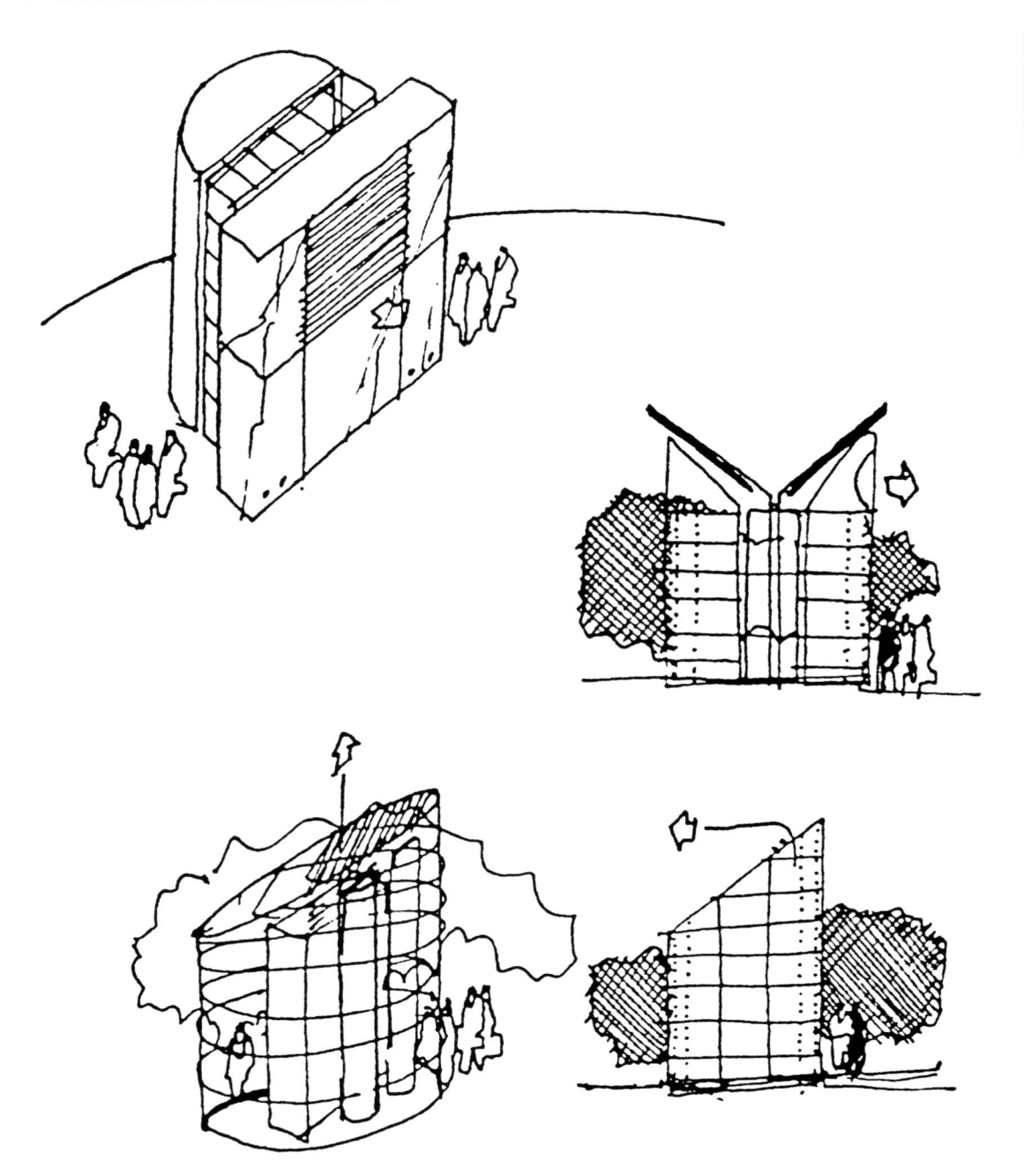

introduced to the seating and handrail details at platform level. A frieze taken from Bermondsey Station was used, and the platform edge doors were standardised across all stations. The lighting feature and services boom that we had designed for the station has been used on several other stations. The concrete 'shoes' fitted to the brick piers to increase their rigidity are unfortunate additions. We would have welcomed the opportunity to propose more sensitive design solutions by introducing cross bracing to the brick piers, but this was outside the scope of our brief. We believe it was a detail the contractor devised during the construction. As we did

not get involved with the stations during the construction phase, it was perhaps inevitable that some of our original ideas would be changed and compromised.

It was a strange experience to witness the completion of a design eight years after the drawings had been issued. Yet what was built was close to the original concept and it was a fantastic project to be involved in.

Civil Engineer: Mott MacDonald
Main Contractor: Costain–Taylor Woodrow

It was perhaps inevitable that some of our original ideas would be changed and compromised.

- BRACKETS SUPPORT CONTINUOUS CABLE BOOM
- CABLE BOOM IS ONLY USED FOR ITEMS IT SUPPORTS
- CABLE BOOM IS NOT USED AS GENERAL CABLE ROUTE (ACCEPT IN SPECIAL CASES)
- CABLE BOOM IS USED AS STRUCTURAL SUPPORT FOR LIGHTS, PA, CCTV, CLOCK & SOME SIGNS. IT MUST BE POSSIBLE TO ADD OR REMOVE THESE ITEMS ANYWHERE ALONG THE ROUTE OF THE BOOM.

sketch: development of
lighting boom
components

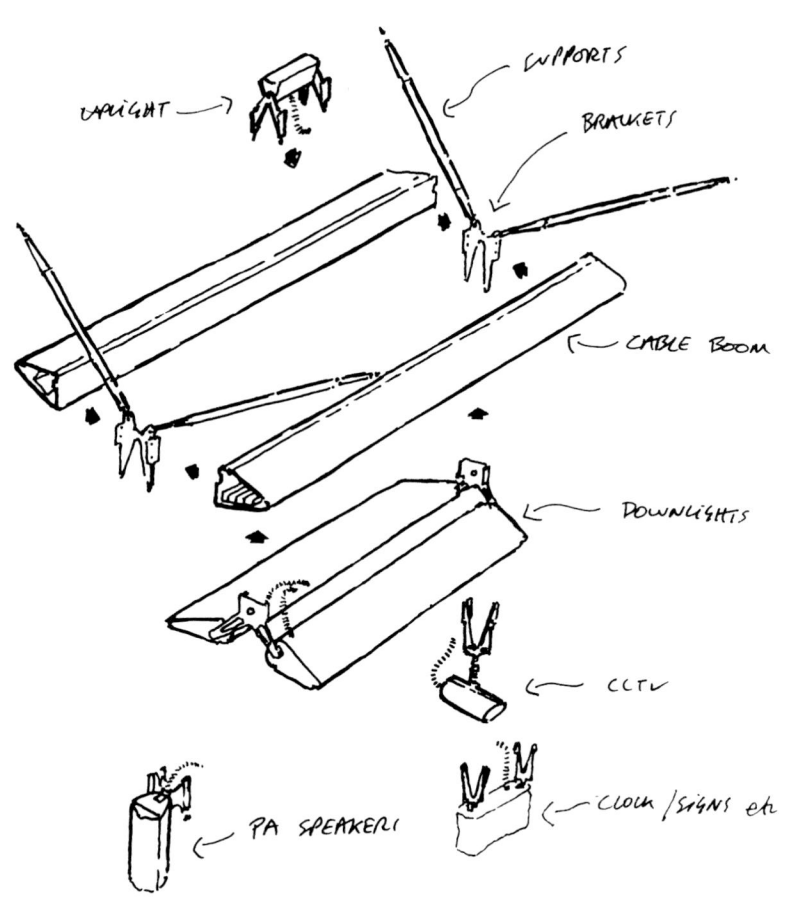

UPLIGHT

SUPPORTS

BRACKETS

CABLE BOOM

DOWNLIGHTS

CCTV

PA SPEAKERS

CLOCK / SIGNS etc

Planning London Bridge Architect: JLE Project Architects

Martin Short, JLE Project Architects

The footpaths were appallingly overcrowded during the rush hour. Recognising this, we demonstrated that the early studies and outline layouts merely dealt with the expansion of the ticket hall and other circulation. Whereas the real problem was passenger flow.

The layout and plan for the two large commuter stations of London Bridge and Waterloo were both resolved by the JLE Project Architects working directly for Roland Paoletti and were as difficult as Westminster to build, though less spectacular. We worked with Weston Williamson on the architectural detailing of London Bridge, but were wholly responsible for the architecture of Waterloo.

It is particularly interesting to look at the evolution of the layout for London Bridge at the surface to see what was generally involved. This is a tidal commuter station with tens of thousands of passengers arriving each hour during the peak period. It stands on a honeycomb of brick vaults extending from Tooley Street to St Thomas Street, thus raising the apparent ground level in the station to that of the viaduct bringing trains to London from the south-east. The vaults on which the station sits were built in the

nineteenth century by several different railway companies, each constructing their part of the combined station at different times, creating different fracture lines where the vault is not continuous.

In 1990 when the design work began, the existing underground ticket hall was an irregular-shaped but tightly-constrained concrete box dropped into the vaulted honeycomb and re-roofed to restore the road level. The only entrances were two sets of stairs from street level and there was a single set of three escalators carrying passengers down from the ticket hall to the southern end of the Northern Line platforms. All passengers leaving the mainline station exited onto the street near the bus station and at that point had to separate into those walking across London Bridge, those going to the underground and those on their way to other destinations whether by bus or foot.

The footpaths were appallingly overcrowded during the rush hour. Recognising this, we demonstrated that the early studies and outline layouts merely dealt with the expansion of the ticket hall and other circulation. Whereas the real problem was passenger flow. Accordingly we set about finding a single all-encompassing solution.

Joiner Street was a busy street connecting St Thomas Street and Tooley Street, slicing its way under the bus station area of the mainline station. It was realised that the new ticket hall would have to be much larger and would spread almost to the flank of the street. A plan of the brick vaults was pieced together from historical drawings and site visits, and this research revealed that there was once a service route through the vaults, from one side of Joiner Street to the other. We surmised that if Joiner Street could be crossed by pedestrians at the

masterplan of station
and access corridors

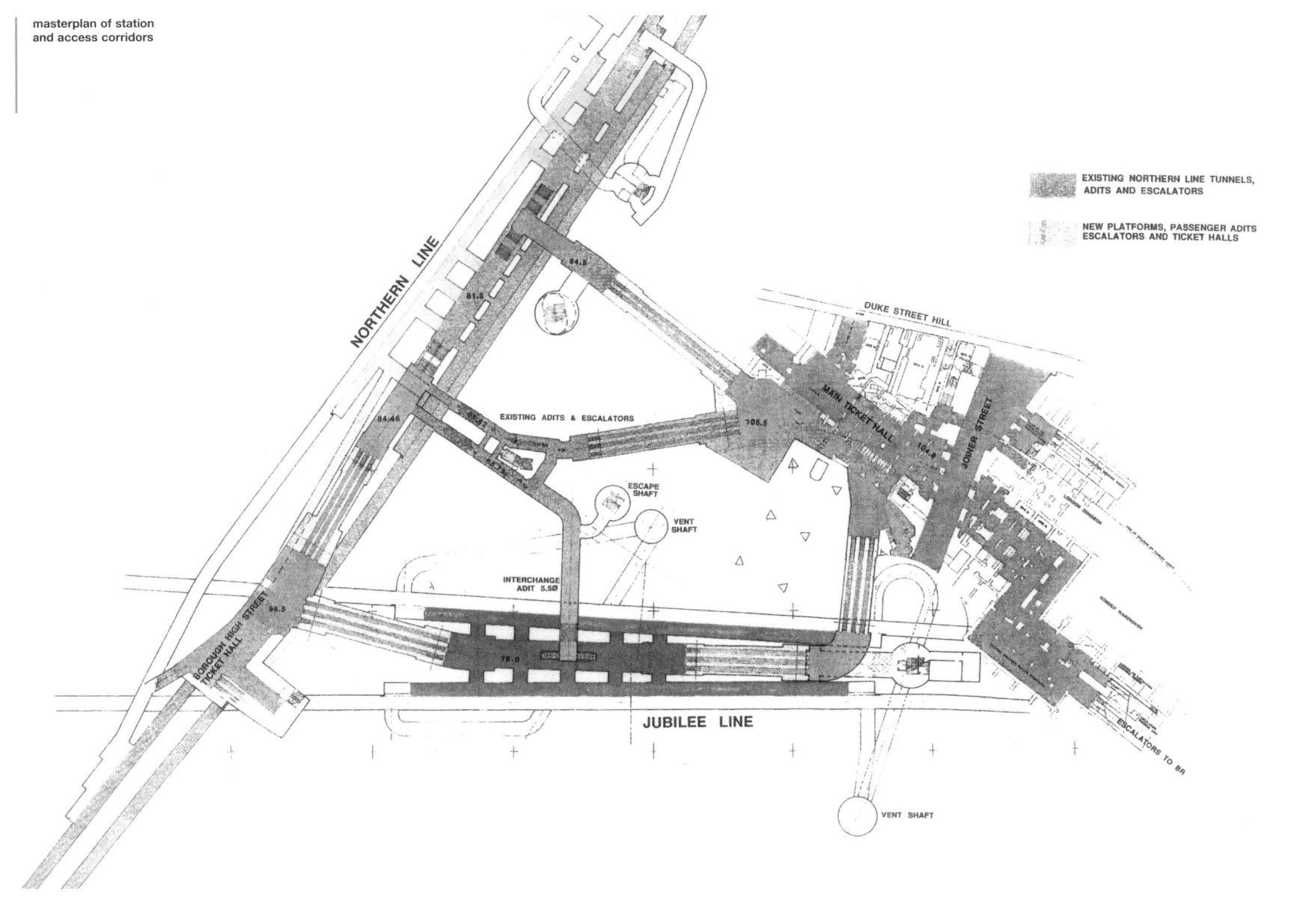

EXISTING NORTHERN LINE TUNNELS,
ADITS AND ESCALATORS

NEW PLATFORMS, PASSENGER ADITS
ESCALATORS AND TICKET HALLS

lower level, which is true ground level, then the large flow of passengers from the mainline and underground station could be separated from other pedestrians, freeing up the surface level for all other circulation. The escalator access would then be within the mainline station so that the original perception of London Bridge being a single railway station, but served by different stairs and escalators, would be restored.

The small 'drop in' box of the 1970s ticket hall would then be extended so that the underground would have a street frontage on Tooley Street and level access from Guy's Hospital in St Thomas Street. The nineteenth century brick vaulting would provide a whole new level of pedestrian movement underneath the overcrowded concourse and bus station forecourt of the mainline station.

Once this idea was conceived it was evolved rapidly – it suggested solutions to all the major problems at London Bridge. However, we faced considerable resistance, particularly from Railtrack, because profitable retail space would be lost, and from Southwark Council, who had to be convinced that it was desirable to close Joiner Street. After several months of persuading and cajoling, it was agreed that it was the right thing to do. The only support at the early stage was from the client body London Underground Ltd who immediately saw the potential of our idea. The most important design innovation at platform level was the link passage between the JLE concourse and Northern Line concourse, which rises out of the JLE concourse. Early studies show a stub shaft containing a spiral stair rising from a central location between the tunnels of the two platforms. The down escalators from

the main ticket hall and Borough High Street ticket hall each have a very restricted concourse that butts up against the stub shaft. We saw a different way of handling this. We observed that it was quite common in smaller, ventilation tunnels to make 90° connections between tunnels. We reasoned that the same method could be used to create an individual T-junction out of the JLE concourse, with stairs rising to a landing level within the concourse and then on up the link passage. It meant that there could be a single JLE concourse passing the Borough High Street escalators to the main ticket hall escalators with the link stairs rising mid-way. All circulation to and from the platforms would pass through this concourse, greatly improving the flow of traffic and allowing passengers who did not know the station an easy and 'tangible' route to the exit.

six

© **Canada Water** Architect: JLE Project Architects with Heron Associates
Commentary by Roland Paoletti

Roland Paoletti explains that this is the only station on the JLE that has been built to the strict engineering economies of the specification typical of a Hong Kong interchange station. Here the concept is taken to a further stage by the architectural device of omitting selected areas of cross slab to create double and triple height vertical space and generally to open up the underground volume. The station has three below-surface levels, the first is a ticket hall, the second level is the platforms for the East London Line and the lowest, the platforms for the Jubilee Line. On the plan all these levels and the differing directions of the two lines are visually held in position by the daylight itself, used as a structuring device, coming from a centrally placed great glazed drum. This great drum of light acts as a beacon for the area.

roof of bus station and glass covered walkway

Despite its substantial appearance, the glazed drum is a simple and economic construction, the frame action of the circular design allowing the steel structure to be both slender and extremely light. The roof overhang is designed to take a suspended metal sunscreening, should it be needed.

Canada Water Station is bisected by two underground lines, the operating line of the East London Line, 11 m below ground level running north–south across the site, and the new JLE line, which, for 22 m of its length runs 8 m below it, in an east–west direction. A large cut-and-cover chasm had to be excavated to build the platforms and track for these two lines. The JLE 'gorge' that was excavated measured 150 m long by 23 m wide and was 22 m deep, while the East London Line required a slot at right angles to it that was 130 m long, 13 m deep and which tapered in width, and had to cradle an active tunnel. The void created in the ground was large enough to swallow St Paul's Cathedral whole and resulted in 120 000 m³ of excavation spoil.

To compound the problem of the cut-and-cover operation, the excavation was sandwiched between a pair of tower blocks at one end and a dock at the other. One side of the excavation ran close to the disused Canada Water Docks and the other came close to the foundations of two existing 22-storey tower blocks. That was not all, the roof slab of the structure had to carry a roadway and the inter-linking bus station, while the box structure of the JLE section had to be capable of supporting a nine-storey air-rights building in the future.

For both the deeper JLE excavation and the East London Line excavation, a secant pile wall enclosure

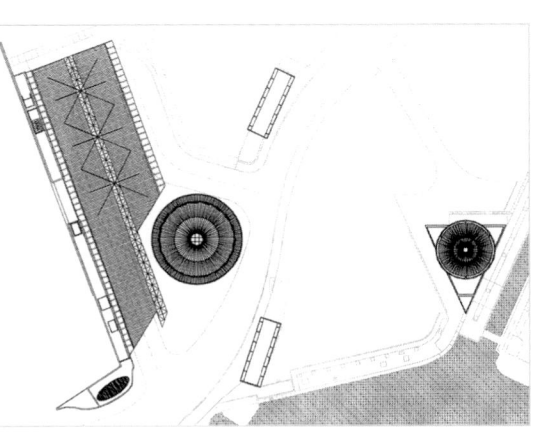

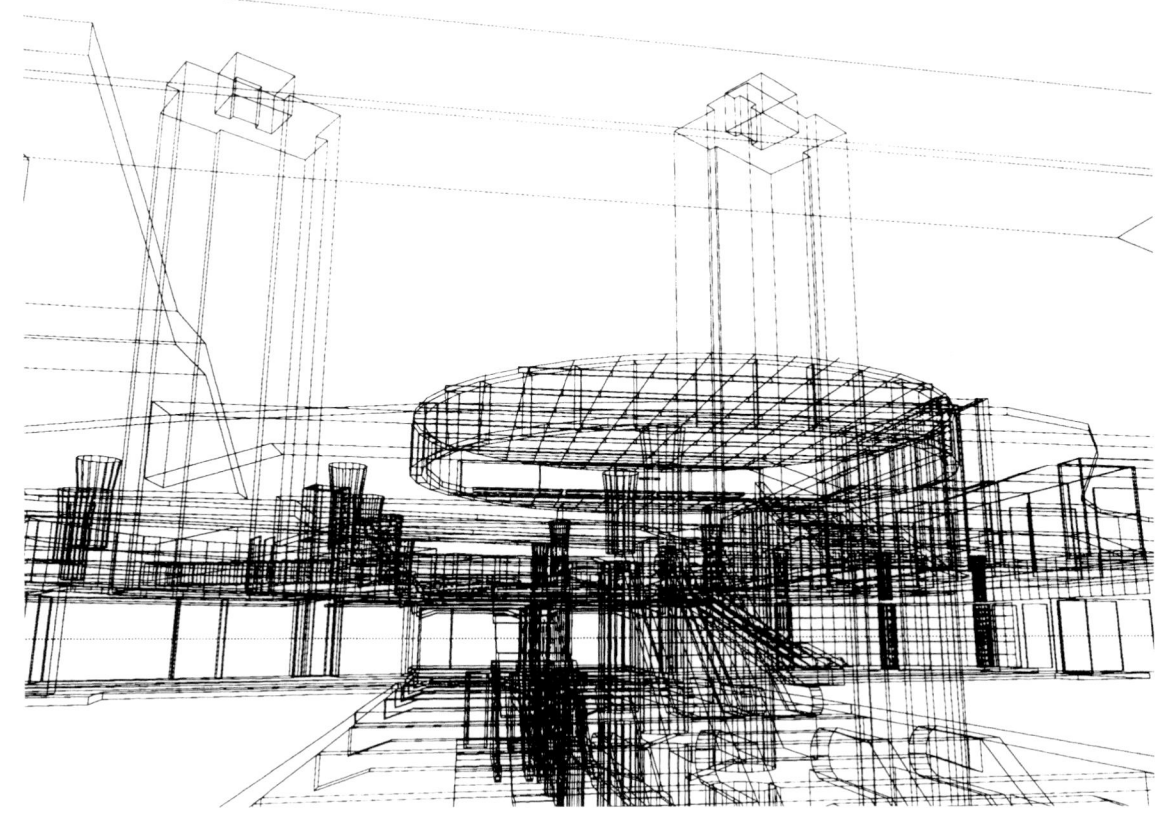

top: large-scale location plan

bottom: plan of station
entrance and bus station

preliminary concept
sketch

One side of the excavation ran close to the disused Canada Water Docks and the other came close to the foundations of two existing 22-storey tower blocks.

entrance rotunda

was chosen, sleeving the top 8 m through made ground and the water-bearing gravel layer. The secant piled wall for the JLE box section was formed by interlocking hard and soft piles of 900 mm and 750 mm diameter respectively, which toe into the Thanet Sands. Tubular steel struts nominally 1 m in diameter were placed across the width of the excavation to brace the piled wall excavation. Each strut was capable of taking a thrust of 1000 tonnes.

Specially made inverted, precast T-beams, were used to form the base of the new box structure, saving on

excavation depth and speeding up construction. The T-beams were in-filled with in situ concrete to form a solid base slab. Where the East London Line bridged the JLE Line, plunge columns were installed into temporary piles to allow construction of the roof to be advanced, ahead of the excavations for the lower JLE platform and tracks.

Following this, the excavation was taken down for the JLE platform and track. The in situ concrete inverted arch of the base slab was formed within the excavation at a depth of 22 m. Flotation of the box structure was resisted by the self-weight of the structure, aided by

entrance shaft

development sketches
of platform

platform level

For the platforms, common access areas, ticket hall and roof, a flat slab was adopted to give maximum headroom, and which spans the width of the box to act as a horizontal prop to the retaining wall.

tension piles anchored into the underlying chalk and by the soil resistance mobilised by extending the arch base slab beyond the line of the retaining wall.

Although the cross section of the deep JLE box varies along its length and is punctured by deep access shafts at each end and a large opening for the station in the roof, a great deal of standardisation was designed into its construction. A stiff, upstand beam runs down the spine of the base slab to help distribute the varying loads acting on the base and to reduce any differential settlement. The upstand beam and adjacent compartment walls also form the service enclosures under the platform that house the essential electrical and other systems that are needed to operate and run the station. For the platforms, common access areas,

ticket hall and roof, a flat slab was adopted to give maximum headroom, and which spans the width of the box to act as a horizontal prop to the retaining wall. The roof slab over the main concourse area was 750 mm deep, to support heavy vehicle loading from the proposed bus station above it. Top-down construction at the west end of the site was adopted to minimise foundation settlements and any ground movement at the nearby tower blocks and to act as an acoustic barrier to minimise construction noise and disturbance

A phalanx of large 1.5 m diameter columns with flared heads, runs the length of the JLE platform and rises 18 m to support the ticket hall floor and roof slab above them. The smooth concrete finish was achieved using metal forms that had been grit blasted to take the shine

It is linked to the underground station entrance by a concourse that is lined with a series of glass-topped 'umbrellas', to shelter commuters walking to and from the station.

axonometric
of station box

off the metal face. Other finishes have been kept simple for practical reasons. Easily cleaned grey mosaic is widely used essentially to cope with the pervading break dust from the East London Line and to provide a homogenous surface covering framed block work and concrete walls alike.

A feature of this and other JLE stations are the glass wall barriers along the platform edges. These ensure that draughts felt by passengers do not exceed the required standard of 5 m/s – tapered tunnel ends are more expensive – keep paper and perishables off the track and make the railway much safer for people on crowded platforms, creating a feeling generally of comfort and security.

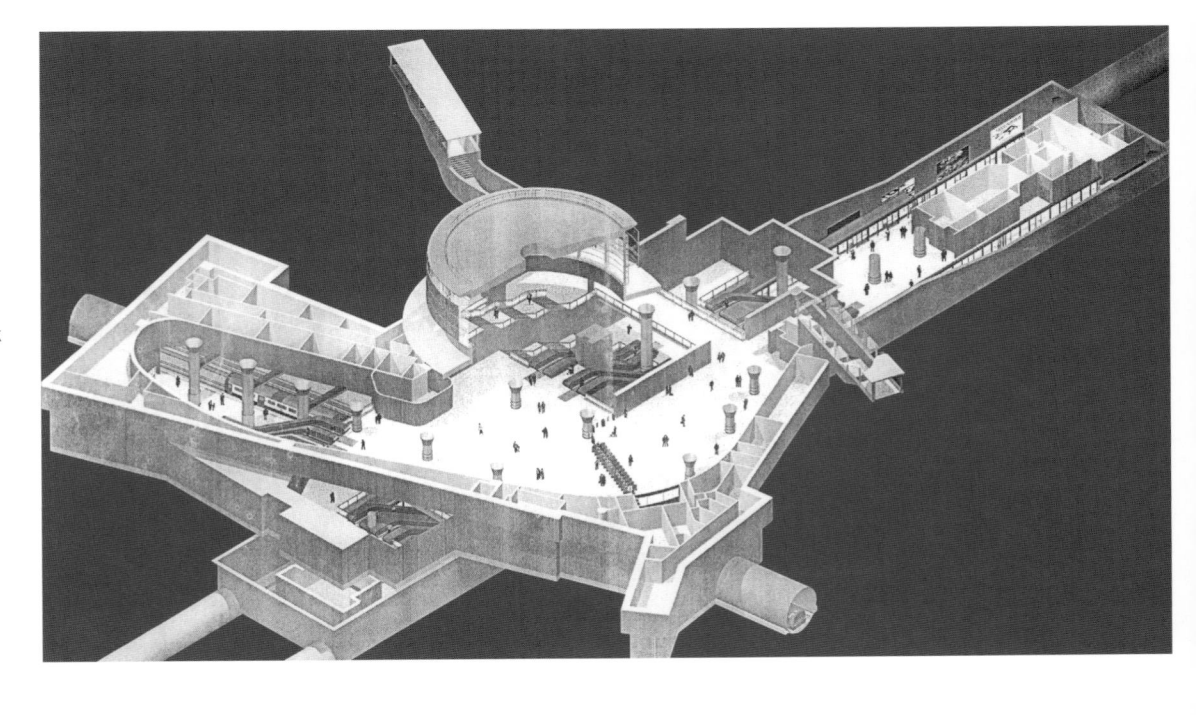

glass walled rotunda and glass covered link

entrance shaft

rendering: access shaft
and escalator

The new bus terminus, adjacent to the glass rotunda of the tube station entrance, is an aluminium and glass clad canopy with a span of 32 m and an overall length of 100 m. It is linked to the underground station entrance by a concourse that is lined with a series of glass-topped 'umbrellas', to shelter commuters walking to and from the station. The aluminium and glass clad wings of the bus station roof cantilever 16 m either side of the roof centreline and comprise a series of steel rib trusses supported on a single row of circular steel columns. The steel structure, the glass fascia and aluminium cladding arrangement, designed by Eva Jericna Architects, creates a smooth, crisp outline reminiscent of the open wings of a sea bird.

Large openings, formed in the roof of the concrete box and at concourse levels, allow daylight to flood into the station and reach deep down onto the platforms.

The new JLE interchange with the East London Line and bus station, opens up new travel links into the City and West End for local residents. The cascading banks of escalators taking commuters to and from the platforms are easily followed and are visible from many parts of the station over its entire length. Large openings, formed in the roof of the concrete box and at concourse levels, allow daylight to flood into the station and reach deep down onto the platforms. Extraordinarily, the under-river tunnels serving the East London Line are in fact Brunel's Thames Tunnel constructed in the 1840s.

Civil and Structural Engineer: Benaim–Works JV
Structural Engineer (glazed drum): Buro Happold
Main Contractor: Tarmac Civil Engineering

seven

© **Canary Wharf** Architect: Foster and Partners

David Nelson and Gerard Evenden, Foster and Partners

It is worth remembering that when we were designing the Canary Wharf JLE Station there was nothing built on Heron Quays, apart from the Docklands Light Railway Station and the low level business units; the built environment was in total contrast to today's now developed urban context of towers. There were always going to be three canopies and a linear garden. Two were large canopies and the third a smaller entrance that became known as the 'Fosterito'.

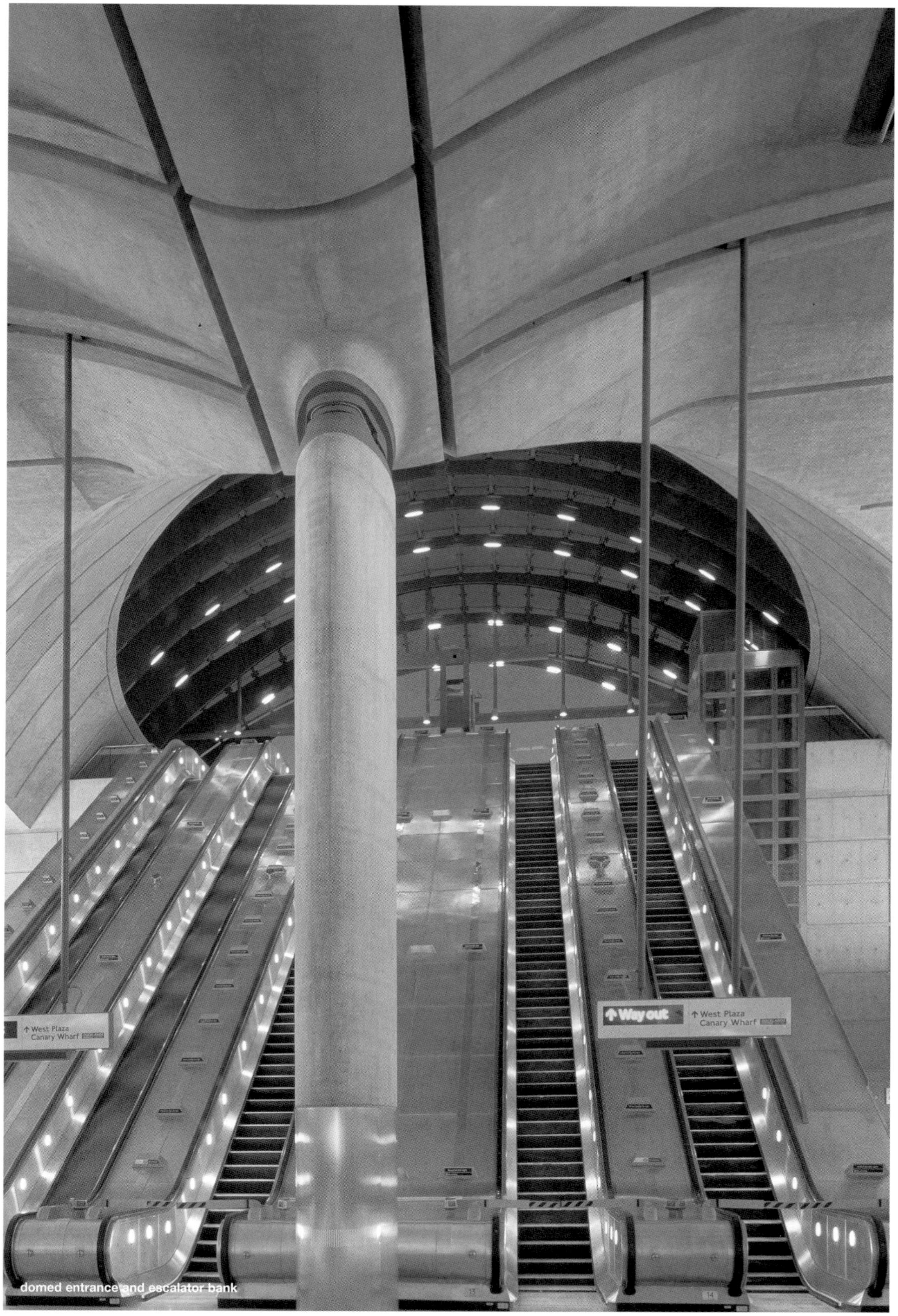

domed entrance and escalator bank

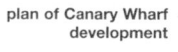

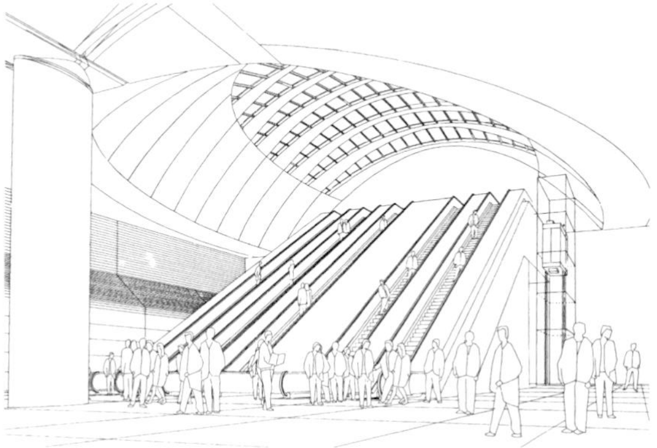

plan of Canary Wharf development

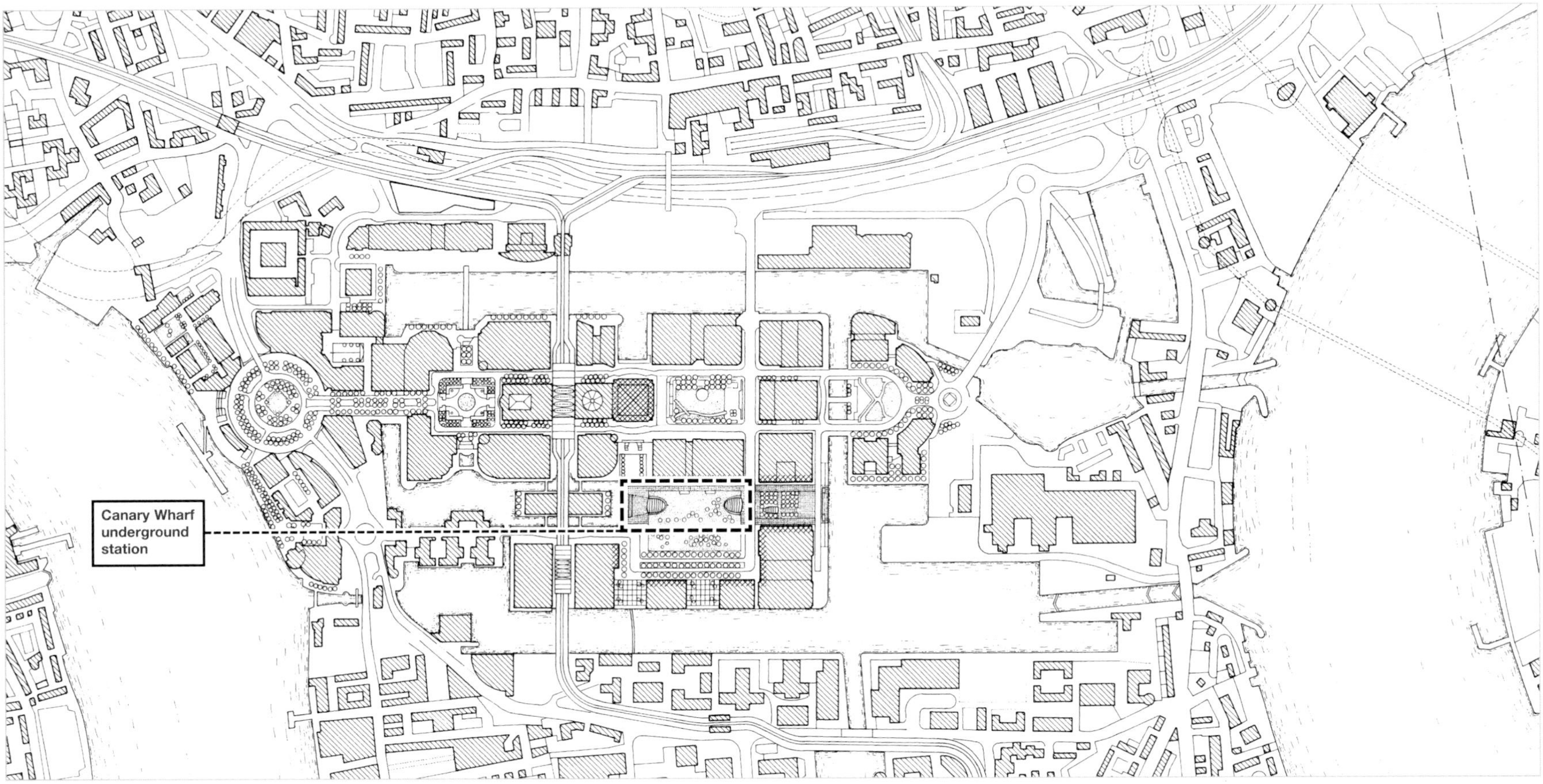

Canary Wharf
underground
station

We must move away from those ceramic tiles beloved by
London Underground, as they fall off, crack and break, and last
about fifteen years. For the walls, we had worked on many
designs using large glass panels to reduce the risk of vandalism.

We had to consider the capacity of the whole
development in 1991, looking to the future when both
Heron Quays and Canary Wharf could be fully occupied.
We have provided enough capacity and flexibility within
the volume of the station box to accommodate further
growth in passenger flow. When the area is fully
developed, Canary Wharf will become the busiest
underground station in the whole network.

The materials chosen for use within the station were
selected as being the most appropriate for the purpose –
low in long-term maintenance and high in durability. The

columns, roof slab and walls, for example, were cast in situ
and have a natural finish, but at their bases, where they can
be touched, the columns are clad in stainless steel to
prevent vandalism and damage. Glass cladding to the
ticket hall cabin and the entrance bubbles was chosen not
only for visibility and to allow natural light into the station
but also for its remarkable resistance to minor vandalism.
The floor is covered in precast concrete pavers.

The choice of the material finishes was simple in our
view. We must move away from those ceramic tiles
beloved by London Underground, as they fall off, crack

and break, and last about fifteen years. For the walls, we
had worked on many designs using large glass panels
to reduce the risk of vandalism. We worked with
J C Decaux on the design of bus shelters, and that
experience showed us that panels of clear glass are less
likely to be vandalised than solid materials; particularly if
the glass is kept clean. This convinced us that we
should use glass to cover the surfaces that people can
touch in the station. We identified a toughened glass,
manufactured by an Italian company called Isiglass, to
glaze the curved canopy at either end of the station.
Isiglass produce armoured glass for the windscreens of

↑ Jubilee line

main roof and centre column supports

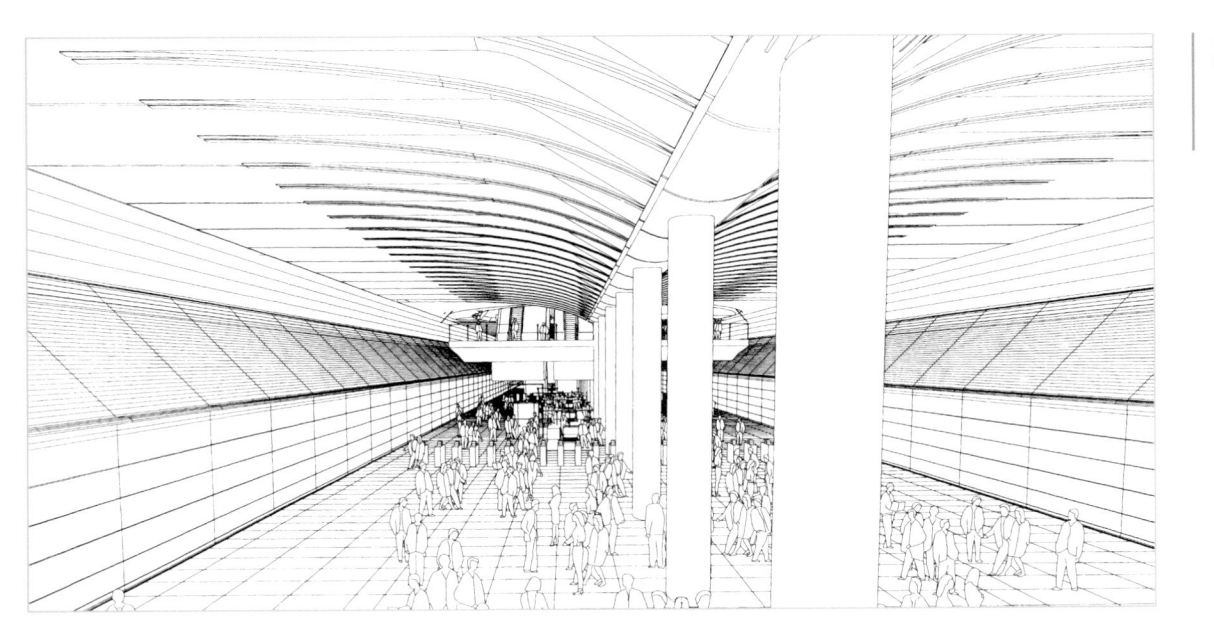

sketch: ticket hall
perspective

So the public areas are a mixture of glass and stainless steel surfaces. The structure of the station is predominantly of reinforced concrete, which has been left exposed where the surface is out of reach.

diagrammatic
longitudinal section

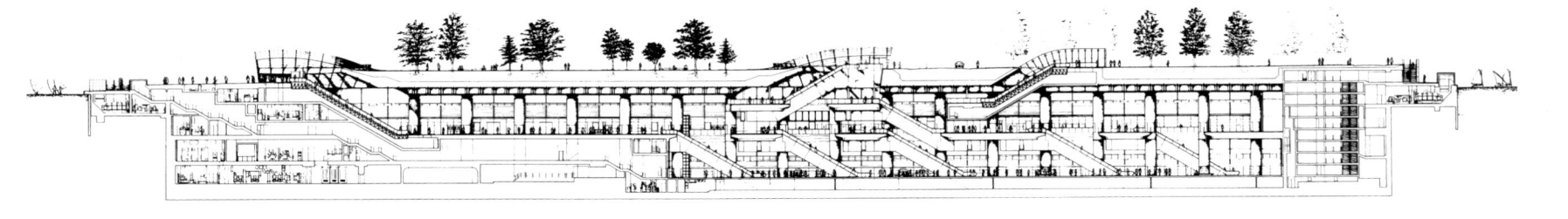

Eurostar trains, Ferrari and Mercedes cars, as well as bullet-resistant glass. They had the technology to curve glass to the accuracy that we required. The double laminated toughened glass for the curved canopy was manufactured in 3 m by 1 m panels and had to withstand vehicle impact. The panel was curved in the longitudinal plane by special bending machines. Each panel was unique and had an exact point on the canopy where it fitted. In all, 76 panels were made, each with a different longitudinal curvature. The glass is held in place

by special spider connections that spring from the thin blade beams arching from the concrete base.

Stainless steel was the other choice for a hard-wearing and durable contact material. Inexpensive powder-coated steel was considered but we were concerned that the powder coating would wear away if rubbed or scuffed by people, luggage and small carts. So the public areas are a mixture of glass and stainless steel surfaces. The structure of the station is predominantly of

reinforced concrete, which has been left exposed where the surface is out of reach. In certain places, where we had to enclose or shroud plant rooms, we used perforated aluminium panelling. The perforations are there for acoustic damping. For the higher walls of the ticket hall we used expanded metal and aluminium framing, to retain the rock wool insulation that is sheathed in a black fabric. The illuminated roundels for the London Underground signs along the platform are twice the size of any roundel on the entire subway

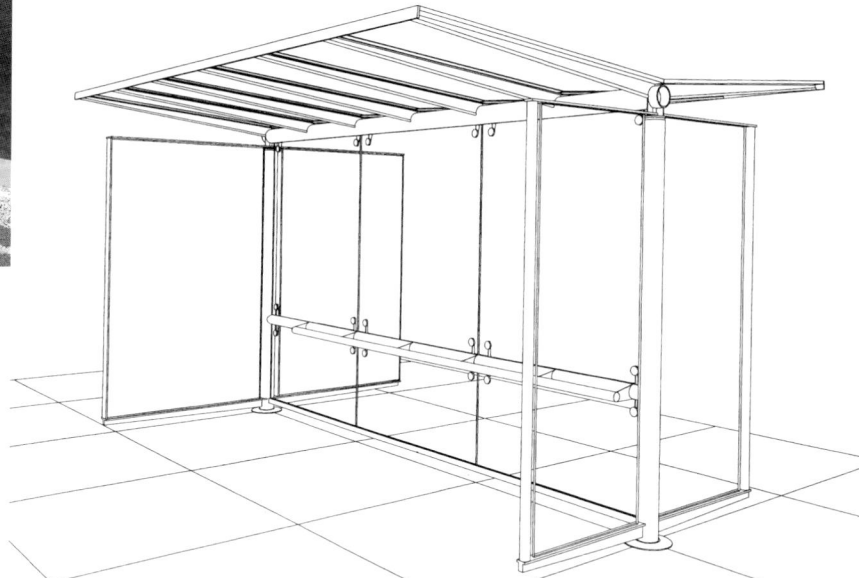

network. They had to be larger to be in proportion with the vast scale of the cut-and-cover box.

The large columns that support the roof of the station are trimmed with 2.1 m-high stainless steel skirtings. The shapes of the columns were originally circular but were squeezed transversely to become ovoid, to ensure that they were slim enough to slot between the escalators without increasing the ticket hall width. The ticket hall has a critical maximum width that allows the station box to fit within the dock, without undermining or encroaching on the dock wall. The elliptical column shape is aesthetically pleasing but was not just fashioned out of architectural whim.

All the exposed concrete has been left with an as-struck finish. The finish colour was light enough to achieve 30 per cent light reflectance. To achieve such a light

We worked with J C Decaux on the design of bus shelters, and that experience showed us that panels of clear glass are less likely to be vandalised than solid materials; particularly if the glass is kept clean.

glass walled entrance

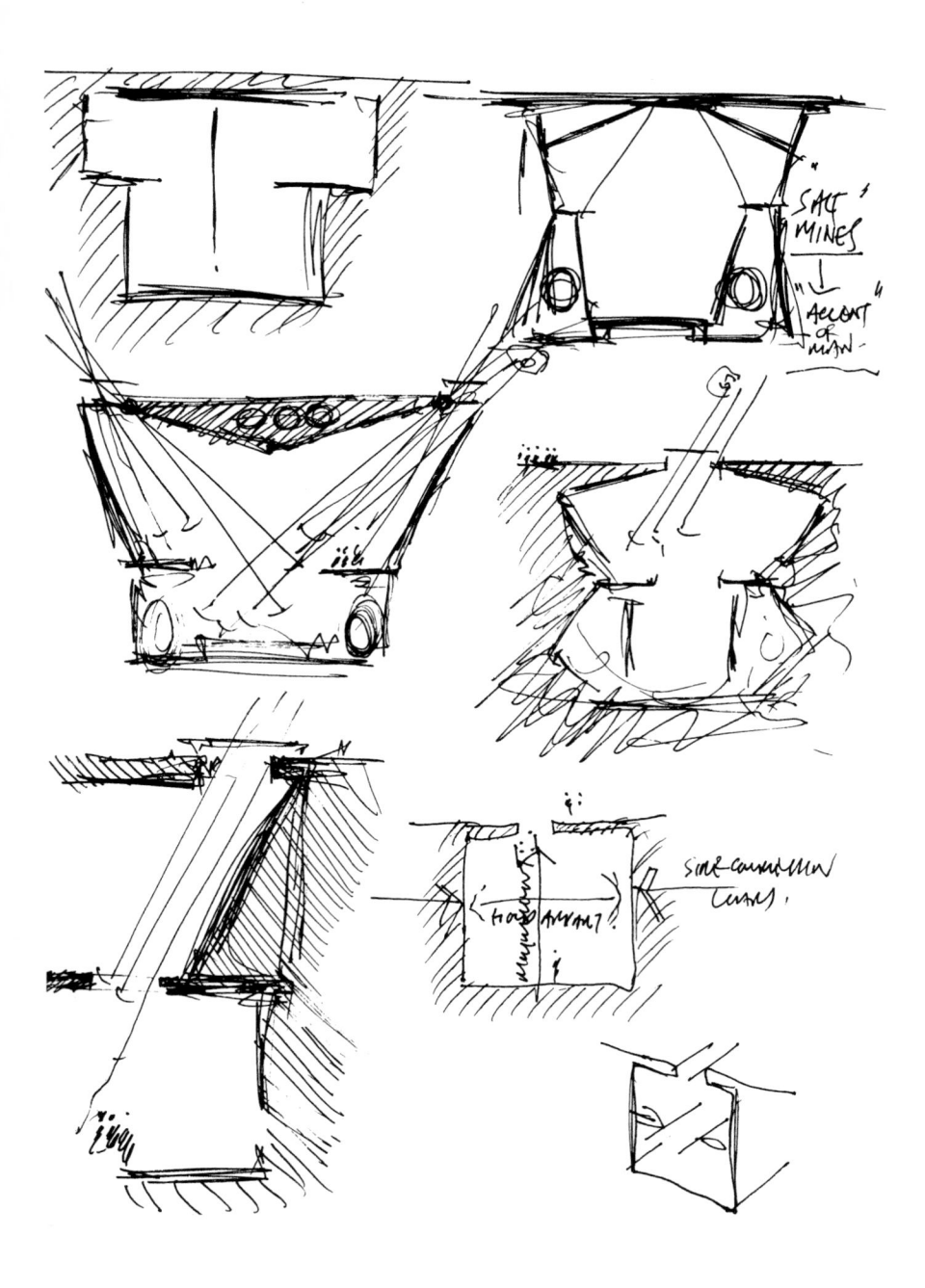

reflective surface using a conventional concrete, we tested the finish of blast-furnace slag cement concrete cast in a variety of shutters – birch faced ply, metal, polymer coated timber. In the end we specified steel shutters for the columns and roof, and birch faced ply for the more complex shapes, particularly the curved base plinth for the entrance canopy. The JLE Engineers wanted to paint the concrete surfaces, believing this would look more finished. Painting the surface means that you have to redecorate it forever. In our offices at Hester Road we regret ever having painted the circular columns because we now paint them at regular intervals, to avoid them looking grubby.

There were very few repairs needed to the concrete surface of the structure. If you repair the as-struck surface the patch will stand out in later years. Generally the surface was rubbed down with a carborundum stone to remove any fins or grout runs and then bagged and washed. A masking mineral-based paint finish was tested on the concrete, but it looked plastic and artificial and was not used.

We used a sixteenth century painting technique of brightening and highlighting the important features of the station to bring them into the foreground. We lit up the surfaces we wanted to be in the foreground and used

dark grey and black colours for those surfaces that we wanted to push into the background and which were not going to be cleaned regularly. More money was spent on the foreground material – glass and stainless steel – and less on the cheap and cheerful background materials. We spent a lot of time deliberating on which surfaces should come to the front or fade into the background. It was the first time that we had consciously expressed a hierarchy of light and darkness for surfaces in this way.

This was the first structure in the whole of the underground network to have a glass lift installed. Of course there was a lot of resistance from the operators,

ticket hall and entrance concourse

We used a sixteenth century painting technique of brightening and highlighting the important features of the station to bring them into the foreground. We lit up the surfaces we wanted to be in the foreground and used dark grey and black colours for those surfaces that we wanted to push into the background and which were not going to be cleaned regularly.

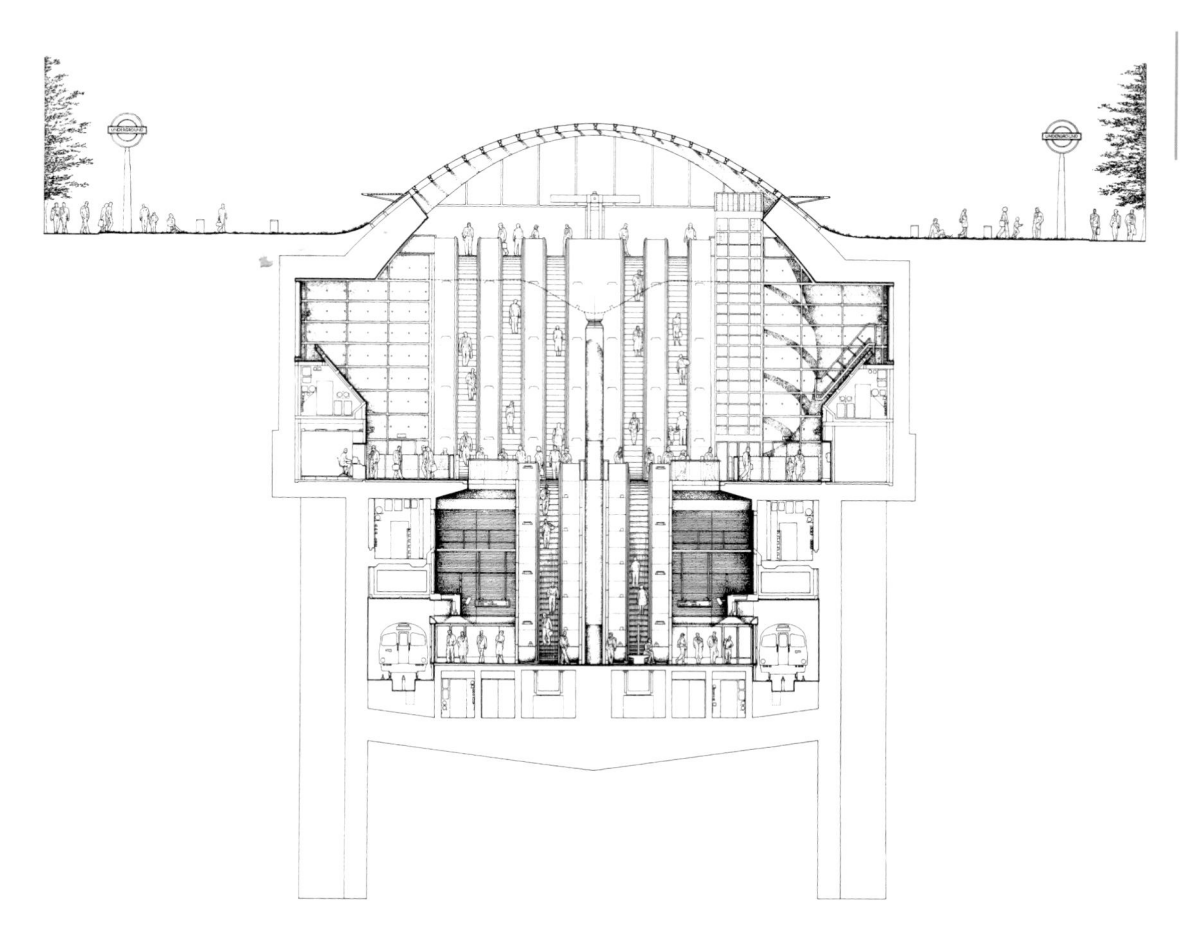

as it created a new precedent that had not been tried before. We won the argument, pointing out that glass would be easier to keep clean and safer for the public because it reduces the risk of crime by its natural visibility.

Our contract from the client was to design just the interior fit-out for the station. We were therefore employed merely as a technical contractor. The project at this stage was compromised due to the Local Authority not allowing the full width of the existing dock to be available for the station. In our earliest discussions with Roland Paoletti and his team we totally agreed with him that this could not be the basis for the ultimate design direction. He allowed us to make proposals, and then instructed us to develop these ideas into a comprehensive scheme. We jointly re-examined the new direction with the authorities, and after considerable effort we were successful in

convincing everyone involved that the station required the full width of the dock.

Although the complexities of engineering the 250 m-long station, within the confines of an historic dock were self evident, the methodology of cut-and-cover construction made possible an appropriate internal scale for the station. The overall design relies on a clear understanding of the key constraints and parameters of the civil engineering work. These include the depth below ground of the trains, the need for a single-level ticket hall, a train crossover zone, and the appropriate methods of construction, in addition to safety and fire protection requirements.

The roof of the station is attached to the retaining walls of the box and is structurally independent of the base

slab and supporting internal columns. The roof sits on sliding bearings at the column supports, to allow for the differential movement. The bearing pads between the roof slab and columns allow the station box to move without inducing large bending forces in the columns. To control uplift and buoyancy of the base slab, 163 tension piles were cast below the base into the Thanet sands. Reinforced concrete elliptical columns rise up from platform level to the roof slab. The green space over the roof of the station was designed to be a miniature parkland with trees, informal shrubs and grass covered banks. It has been altered by the Canary Wharf developers into a formal garden with a piazza.

Within the long box structure we have aimed to give the traveller a direct and smooth progression from street level down to the ticket hall, then down again to the

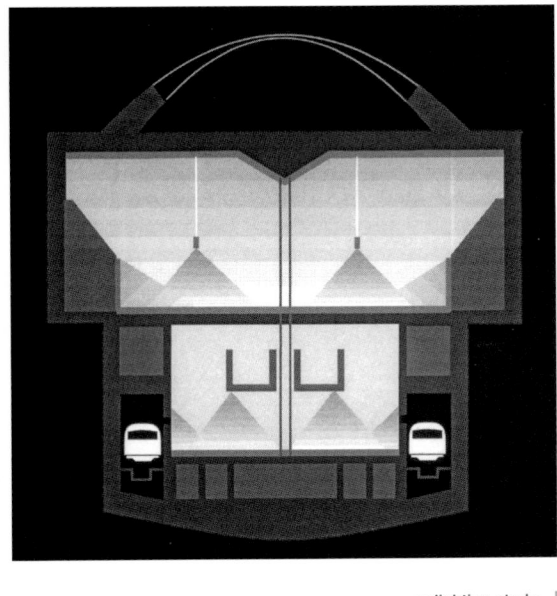

uplighting study

Natural light is focused at the two main entrances, through large glazed domed canopies. Each dome spans 20 m and is carefully integrated into the sloping grass banks at either end of the new park that will be the principle recreation space for all of Canary Wharf. By concentrating natural light at these points, the direction of passenger movement is made clear without signage, when using any of the 19 escalators.

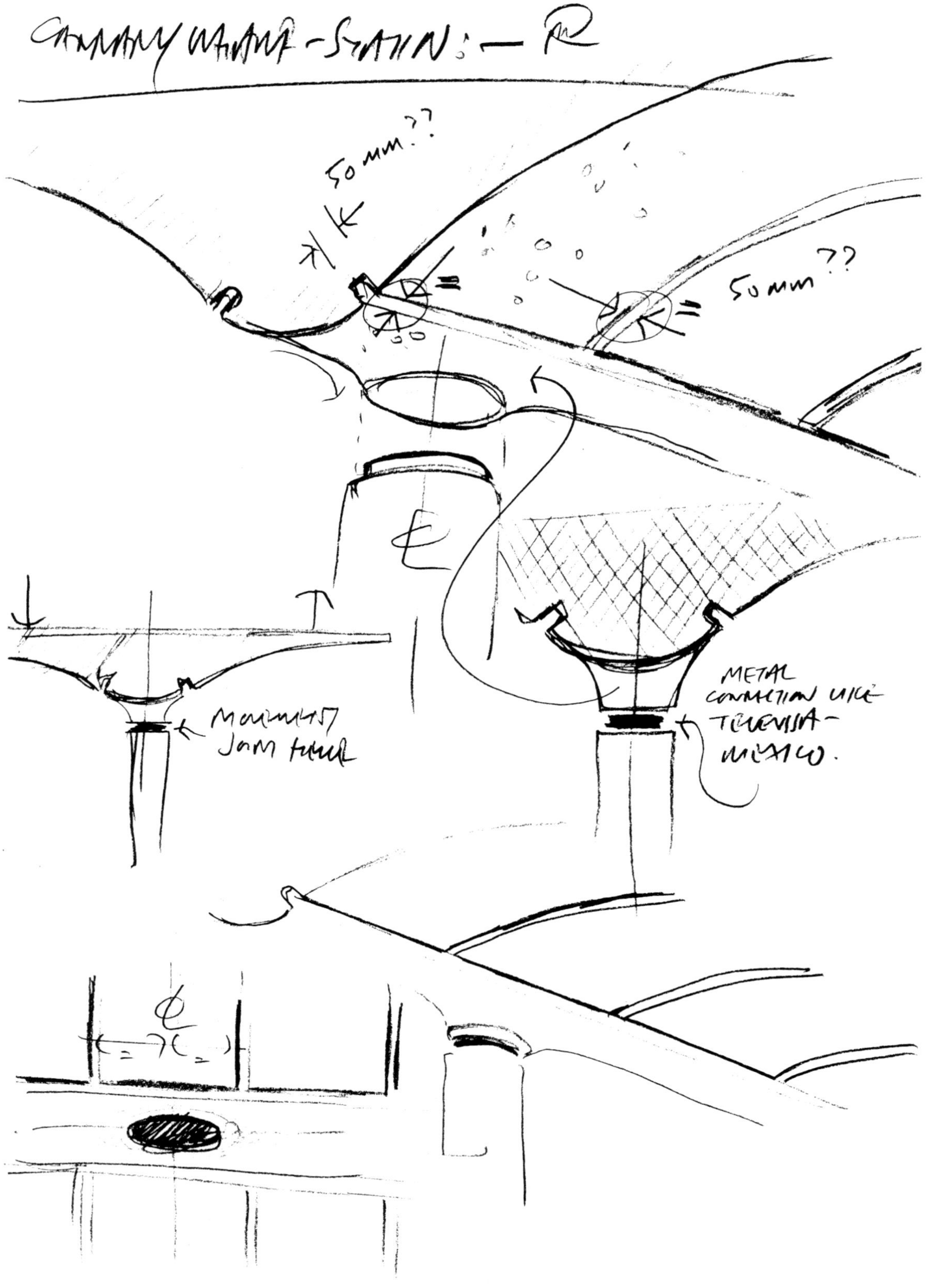

CANARY WHARF - STATION :— R

50 mm ??

50 mm ??

MOVEMENT JAM HALL

METAL CONNECTION LIKE TELEVISA — MEXICO.

modelling the roof and column junction

Canary Wharf Station has been designed on the collective human scale to accommodate the inevitable increases in passenger density that future generations will experience.

trains. Natural light is focused at the two main entrances, through large glazed domed canopies. Each dome spans 20 m and is carefully integrated into the sloping grass banks at either end of the new park that will be the principle recreation space for all of Canary Wharf. By concentrating natural light at these points, the direction of passenger movement is made clear without signage, when using any of the 19 escalators.

Administrative offices, plant kiosks and other amenities are sited along the flanks of the ticket hall for flexibility and ease of maintenance. This leaves the main internal volume free, giving the station its clarity and visibility. Claude Engle, an international lighting consultant, was responsible for all lighting that you see at Canary Wharf Station. His idea was to create an artificial sky on the ceiling of the roof, which would throw light down onto the ticket hall to create a well-lit space by day and night. Daylight from the entrance canopy will not be quite such a blinding contrast

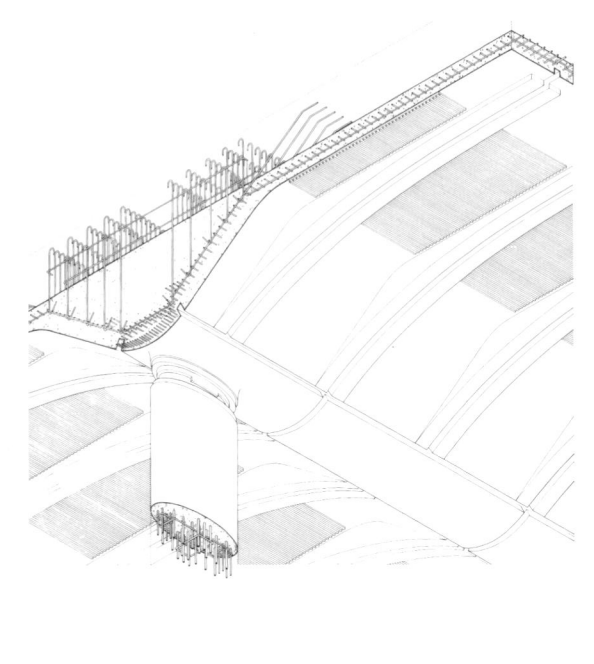

on entering the ticket hall and on gloomy overcast days the spread of reflected light will be a bonus.

We can still enjoy the collective gathering experience. Stations are meeting places, places of interaction and a crossroads in our hectic lives. By creating soaring volumes of space within the station we can remain individuals without feeling congested or claustrophobic no matter how close we are to our neighbours. Canary Wharf Station has been designed on the collective human scale to accommodate the inevitable increases in passenger density that future generations will experience. The completed buildings of Canary Wharf already give a foretaste of its scale, density, and strategic importance to London as a whole.

Civil Engineer: Posford Duvivier
Main Contractor: Tarmac Bachy Joint Venture

ovoid central column and sliding bearing

eight

© **North Greenwich** Architect: Alsop Architects (formerly Alsop Lyall & Stormer)

Will Alsop, Alsop Architects

When people talk about buildings and structures, they consider architecture as something that is applied to it. That is a terrible development in our vocabulary. Everything is architecture – both good and bad. In my book good architecture is when there is some element of delight perceived by the people that use a public building or space. With North Greenwich Station it is those people operating it and the travelling public. In order to create good architecture certain qualities are needed. One should be educated in structures and how they behave. It is not possible to have a meaningful dialogue with engineers without a grasp of structural form.

elevated walkway, main concourse

preliminary concept
sketch

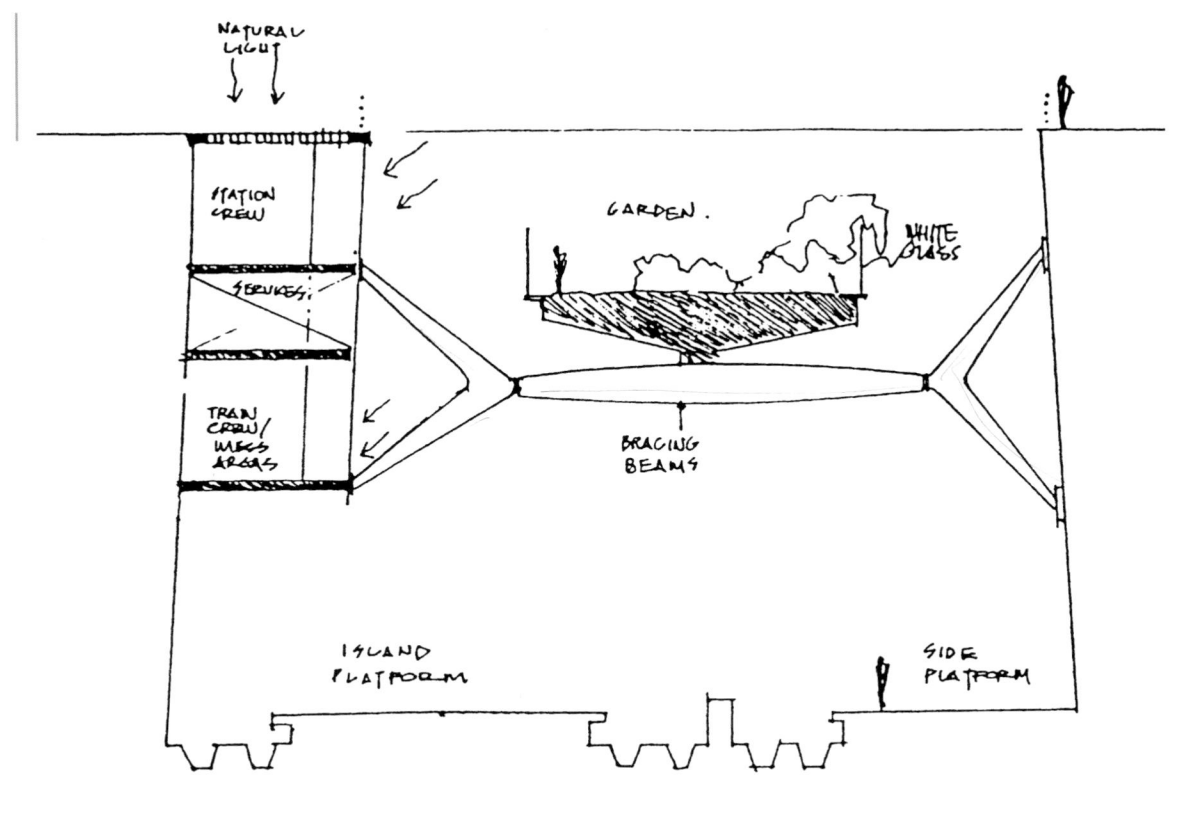

It is a process of discovery, not about the grand conception nor the architecture or engineering and how it must be, but about throwing up a range of ideas and possibilities.

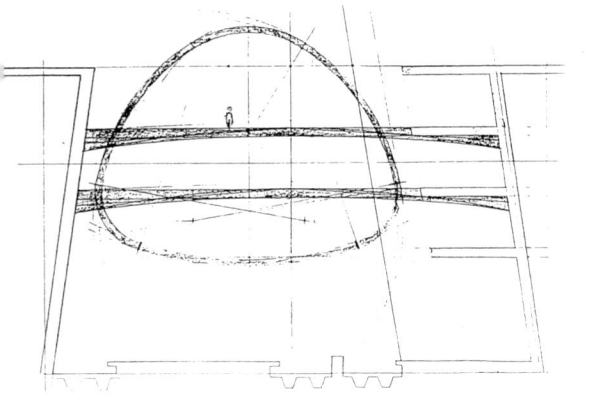

I was lucky enough to be introduced to structural design as a student at the AA in a very positive way: there was a whole series of education and learning experiences on pneumatic and tensile structures and folded plates. And sometimes in order to get a feel for the 'tension' and 'compression' forces and understand their behaviour, we erected human pyramids with our fellow students. We should consider a design not just as a work of civil engineering but as a piece of architecture as well and be able to have intelligent three-dimensional conversations with engineers using line drawings, CAD images and models to better understand what we are trying to do. It is a process of discovery, not about the grand conception nor the architecture or engineering and how it must be, but about throwing up a range of ideas and possibilities.

Before we became involved with North Greenwich there was already a JLE briefing document stating that it was to be a cut-and-cover station with a roof slab. When we teamed up with Benaim-Works we explored various ideas for the station. I suggested that we should omit the roof slab and open the station to the sky. I developed the idea further with sketches and even models before presenting it to the client, who initially accepted it. As an open station we had a 400 m long box, 30 m high and 25 m wide. It contained a sharp edge on the surface, which we could put a handrail around so that when you look down into it you can see the trains running through. There would be a need to put smaller buildings within it for ticket offices and administration and so on – we thought this was a terrific idea. Economically of course we save

Economically of course we save money by eliminating a slab on the top for the roof, but the biggest saving comes from eliminating the ventilation ducts and shafts that would be required for an enclosed station.

money by eliminating a slab on the top for the roof, but the biggest saving comes from eliminating the ventilation ducts and shafts that would be required for an enclosed station. It seemed to me that the quality of the station environment would be better because you could see the sky and there would be greater security for the public using the station because it was full of open spaces. The way that the scheme developed was that you would descend 5 m from ground level down to the ticket office then walk along a bridge longitudinally, which was designed like a terrace garden, before you took the

escalator to platform level. It is exactly the organisation of space that we have now built, except that the station has a roof. I remember working with Benaims and discussing how we should stop the freestanding side walls from imploding – do we have to have cross beams to strut the walls? Can we design the walls with a sinusoidal profile for greater freestanding rigidity?

Our proposals in the end had to be put before British Gas who owned the land. At the time there was no Millennium Dome, and British Gas were happy to have a

station because it would increase the value of their land, as they thought there were going to be housing and offices on it. They saw the open station as the centrepiece of the development and went along with our ideas even wanting to rename the station 'Port of Greenwich' which was the name of their development site. That is sadly as far as it got. Shortly after that we received instructions from JLE that the roof had to go back on because there was a strong possibility of building over the station sometime in the future. Nevertheless, we had gained from our experience, and

model of the open station

concept sketch

carried forward the design philosophy of the clean 'open' box. There are advantages in having fewer columns at platform level and less pile cap bases to build, and close-centred columns from which to suspend the concourse slab and to support the roof. The solution was a logical one and came from engineering efficiency. The visual delight is in the quality of the surface colour and profiled shape of the concrete columns.

Concrete as an aesthetic material has been treated with suspicion by many architects and I am among the

91

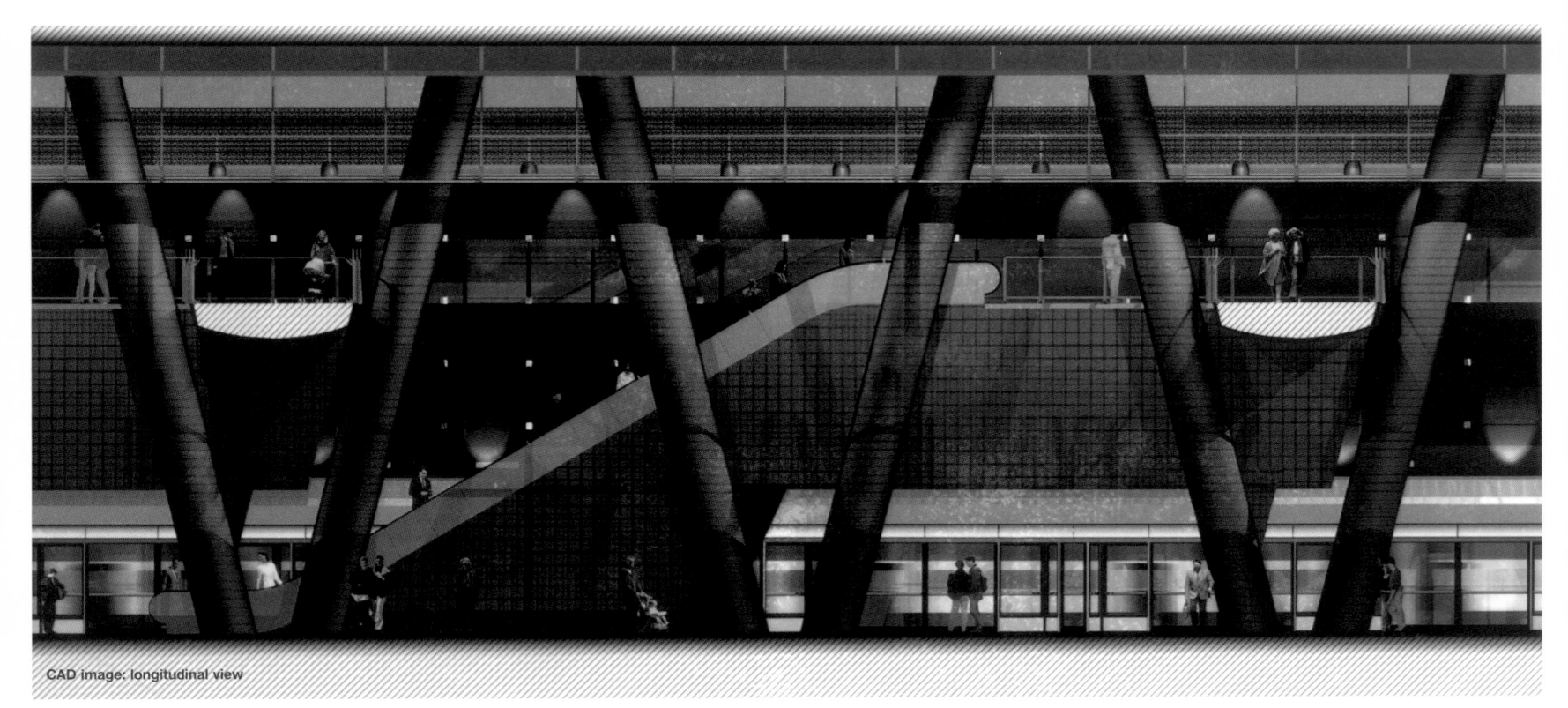

CAD image: longitudinal view

concept sketch

I was not thinking about the cost but the right colour at the time, and in my defence I would say that the major cost is surely in the manufacture of terrazzo and tiles, not in the raw ingredients.

non-believers. Why is this? It is true that I have not used much exposed concrete, although on North Greenwich I was extremely impressed with the in situ finish of the concrete columns. It was a surprise for me because I did not think the UK construction industry could achieve that quality of finish. French contractors on the other hand can produce very good site-cast concrete. The cruciform legs on the building in Marseilles are just painted site-cast concrete, and the quality is superb.

Undoubtedly the 'Piranesi Blue' columns give the station its dramatic effect, but my critics say how can I justify the cost of those highly polished mosaic tiles and terrazzo,

using cobalt pigments (the most expensive money can buy) and still be in budget? I was not thinking about the cost but the right colour at the time, and in my defence I would say that the major cost is surely in the manufacture of terrazzo and tiles, not in the raw ingredients. Remember that the terrazzo surfaces and mosaic tile coverings were specified by JLE and I was working to the brief. A lot of people say that I am fixed on blue after I designed the Marseilles Building, but it was not blue until relatively late in the design development. We had chosen the blue for North Greenwich well before Marseilles, and I know that having done so it did influence my decision to go for blue on Marseilles.

In my view it had to be blue, as it was an enclosed box and I was trying to create a feeling of endless space rather than confinement. That is why the undersurface of the ceiling to the roof is not really finalised but there is a hint of it as you see through it and the blue glass wall beyond. It gives the notion that it goes on into infinity. The reason I like blue is its deep colour, its deadness and the way it absorbs the light like a black hole. It is the same sort of colour tone as a deep-copper beech tree that contrasts with the fresh green of a horse chestnut tree in May and this wonderful copper colour sucks all the light in and is not read as a three-dimensional form, but as a black hole.

splayed columns rise to the roof

We were appointed by the JLE organisation on the recommendation of Roland Paoletti and were appointed after making a successful fee tender bid. We did bid rather low, partially through naivety and because we wanted the job. The budget that we had to work with was negligible compared to the civil engineering cost. As it turned out the architectural budget – not our fee – was 10 per cent of the total contract value and we were within budget. We did everything up to tender. The overruns and over spending were more to do with the way the project was contracted, than anything else. The JLE organisation worked on the basis that everything was going to be confrontational and so we all became adversarial. Up to

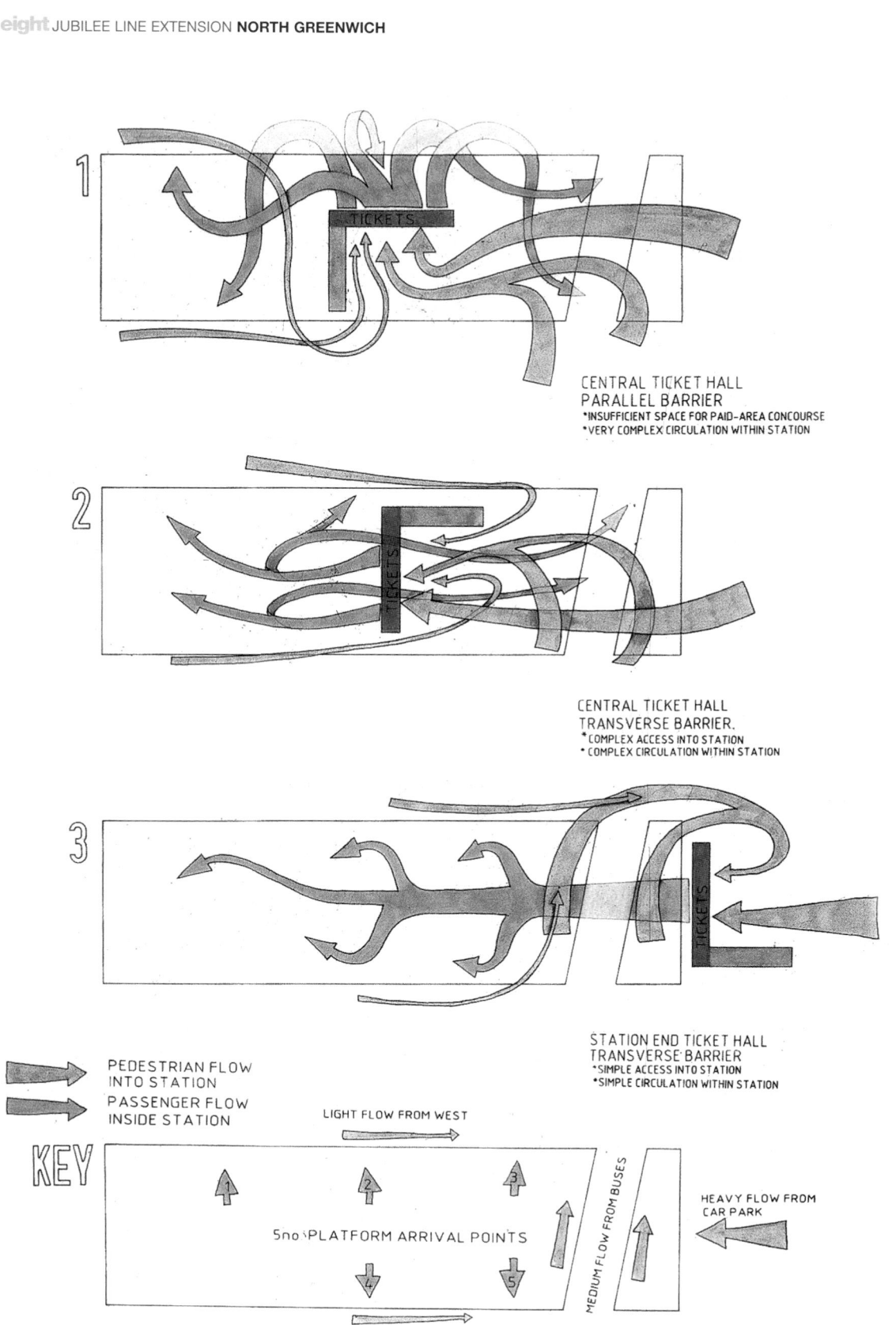

CENTRAL TICKET HALL
PARALLEL BARRIER
*INSUFFICIENT SPACE FOR PAID-AREA CONCOURSE
*VERY COMPLEX CIRCULATION WITHIN STATION

CENTRAL TICKET HALL
TRANSVERSE BARRIER.
* COMPLEX ACCESS INTO STATION
* COMPLEX CIRCULATION WITHIN STATION

STATION END TICKET HALL
TRANSVERSE BARRIER
*SIMPLE ACCESS INTO STATION
*SIMPLE CIRCULATION WITHIN STATION

PEDESTRIAN FLOW
INTO STATION

PASSENGER FLOW
INSIDE STATION

KEY

LIGHT FLOW FROM WEST

5no PLATFORM ARRIVAL POINTS

MEDIUM FLOW FROM BUSES

HEAVY FLOW FROM
CAR PARK

LIGHT FLOW FROM WEST

In the end I feel the architecture is only as good as the client! If Roland Paoletti had not been part of the JLE, life would have been impossible for architects. We would not have been appointed and even if we had it might have been very difficult to get our ideas accepted.

tender stage, while working with our consultants things went very well. We were to budget and on time – the only problem was in dealing with the services, which had not been finalised. I think that was a disaster, as the services represent a large part of the overall station budget. The services contract was dealt with internally by JLE and was not developed to the same level of finished detail as the architecture and structural design when we went out to tender. If you go backstage to North Greenwich you will find a number of empty rooms fully decorated but with nothing in them, which should have taken services plant. Perhaps some of those rooms are for future capacity such as the possible branch line to the Royal Docks and City Airport. The late appointment of Drake and Scull as design and build services contractor meant that any savings in space and capacity could not be recovered. In normal circumstances if they were part of

view at platform level

the design team, we would have caught wind of that and tried to give that volume back to the public areas. As our role ended at tender stage, we had no input during the construction phase.

In the end I feel the architecture is only as good as the client! If Roland Paoletti had not been part of the JLE, life would have been impossible for architects. We would not have been appointed and even if we had it might have been very difficult to get our ideas accepted. We would consult with Roland to seek his advice on impending problems and he in turn would help our case by arguing it through on the client side.

Civil Engineer: Benaim-Works
Contractor: Sir Robert McAlpine

nine

◎ **Canning Town** Architect: Troughton McAslan

Nick Eldridge, Eldridge Smerin Architects (formerly Troughton McAslan) and
Greg McClean, John McAslan Architects

Canning Town is a transport interchange located in the heart of East London, comprising six platforms for trains and a fourteen-stand bus station carefully integrated within a confined finger of land between Silvertown Way and Bow Creek.

Troughton McAslan was appointed as architect for the new station with WSP Kenchington Ford as lead consultant. Our joint role as 'Technical Contractor' is a term architects are less familiar with. It is true to say that, under this contract, our authority to maintain the quality standard of the construction was reduced.

row of 'V' columns supporting the DLR

However, from the outset, we understood that the JLE Head of Design, Roland Paoletti, wanted bold, innovative design and sought out a few architects who did not necessarily have a background in station design and who would bring fresh ideas to the project.

The original brief we were given in June 1991 required a bus station linked, by a bridge and high-level concourse, to the Jubilee Line and DLR platforms, which were positioned side by side. Although the North London Line (NLL) ran parallel to the JLE, the existing NLL station was to remain separate from the new interchange. The site was on a confined space with the presence of high-tension power lines running over the northern section prohibiting the use of conventional tower cranes for lifting and erecting the structure. We therefore had to

plan the station within a narrow strip of land, constrained by Bow Creek to the west and the road of Silvertown Way to the east. To clear the sag of the 400 kV power line, the height of the structure was restricted to 7 m above ground. It was not practical to reposition the pylons nor re-route the power line.

The concourse of the first scheme, CAT 1, was supported on V-shaped, splayed, concrete columns. The geometry of these supports was generated by the incline of the escalators that linked the concourse to the JLE platforms below. This device gave the station structure a strong dynamic expression, which was appropriate for a transport building and a personality by which the station could be recognised.

As the escalators needed independent maintenance, precast concrete Vierendele spine beams were connected below the DLR concourse level, to facilitate access. From the beams we hung all the plant and services provision for the station. By suspending the modular service pods from the DLR concourse we provided a flexible system enabling future expansion and addition of more service pods as well as a dedicated route for maintenance staff beneath the concourse.

Our civil engineering partners WSP fully supported the design concepts that we proposed. Although our estimated sizing of certain structural elements was perhaps optimistic and was later enlarged, the overall visual balance of the V-section has remained. We opted

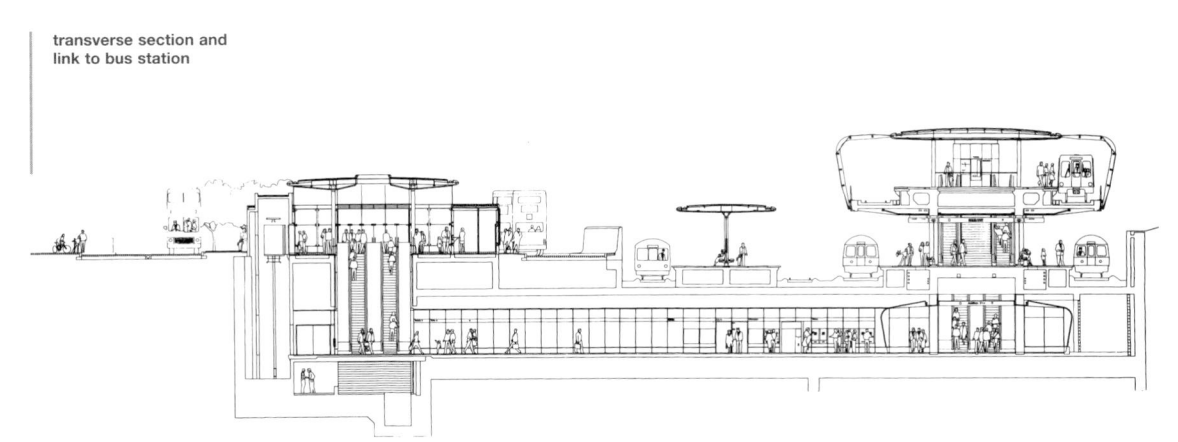

design development
drawing: row of 'V'
columns supporting
the DLR

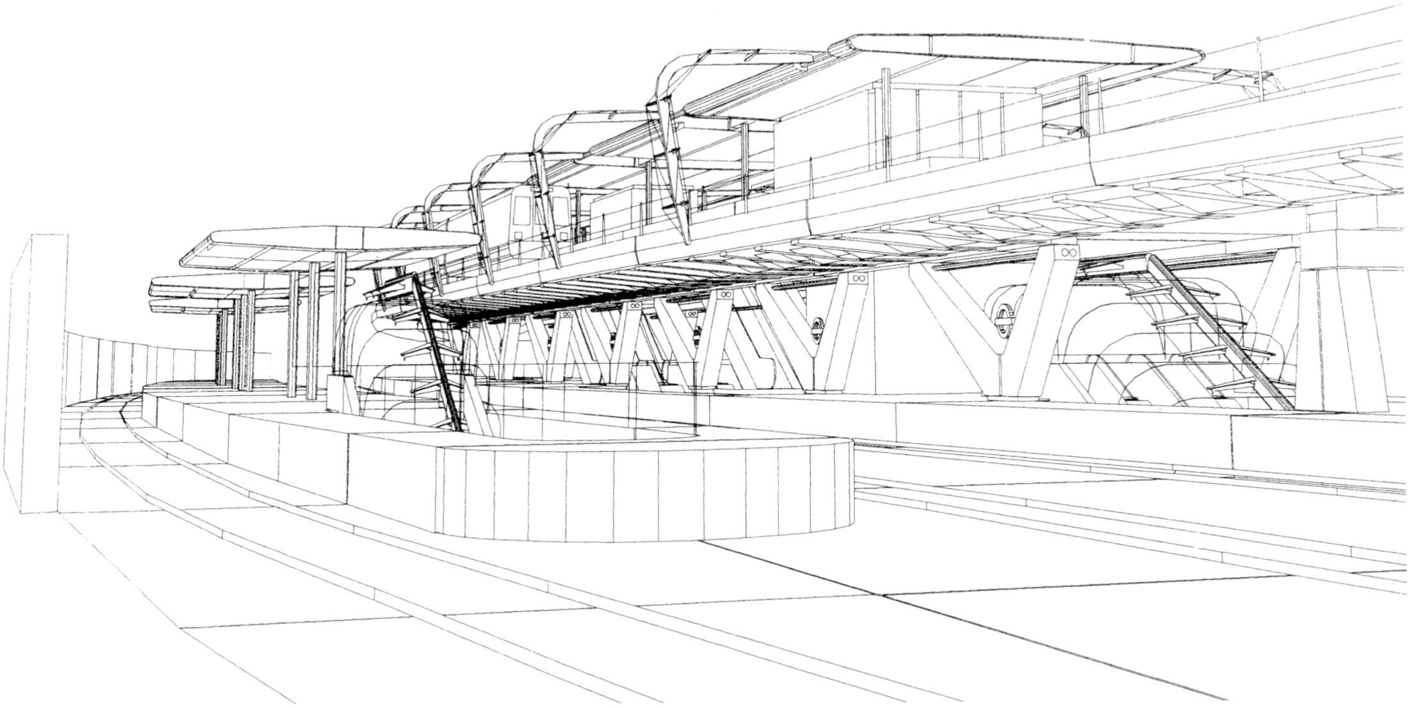

The site was on a confined space with the presence of high-tension power lines running over the northern section prohibiting the use of conventional tower cranes for lifting and erecting the structure.

for wide, shallow beam elements, which would look slimmer than deep, narrow beams. A structural tie was introduced at the top of the splayed columns for robustness. The ties have been expressed as macalloy rods with sheaths for protection. We were keen to articulate and express the structure, repeating the rhythm of the splayed columns, service pods and escalator arrangement along the length of the station.

In October 1991, when we had finalised the first scheme, CAT 1, we received a new brief to integrate the North London Line within the new station plan. We had about two weeks working with a new partner, Maunsells, to provide information for the funding approval of this revised scheme and worked with Maunsell to convert the original design. In December, a

transverse section and
link to bus station

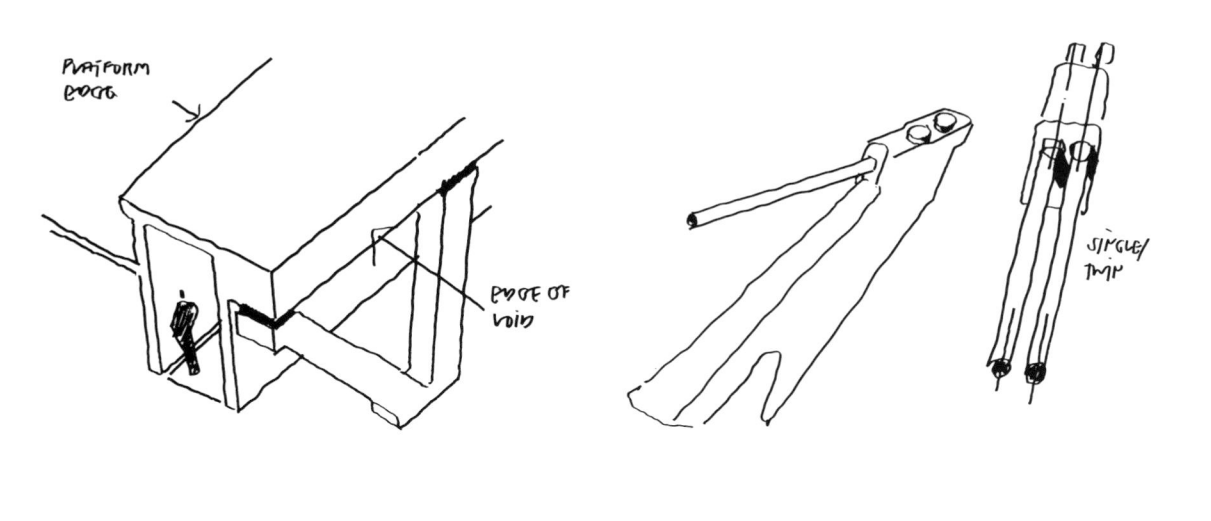

The practical solution now was to vertically integrate the two stations – with the DLR now running above the JLE track – and to push the concourse into the ground to clear the overhead power lines. This necessitated a major re-alignment of the existing DLR track in order to achieve a symmetrical stacking of the concourse, and the JLE and DLR platforms.

month later, we were advised that WSP, our original partners, had been reappointed, having successfully re-bid the design work! This change of engineers mid-design added complexity and a degree of confusion. We put an immense amount of effort into re-planning a complex project and trying to salvage the essence of the previous scheme which we felt was well resolved and architecturally very exciting.

The practical solution now was to vertically integrate the two stations – with the DLR now running above the JLE track – and to push the concourse into the ground to clear the overhead power lines. This necessitated a major re-alignment of the existing DLR track in order to achieve a symmetrical stacking of the concourse and

the JLE and DLR platforms. The original design, without the North London Line link, had greater clarity. We had achieved a balanced expression of the structure and the services. In the revised scheme, CAT 2, the service elements were located out of sight, buried alongside the underground concourse. With the revised scheme we extended the V-shaped structures down below ground so that they became a Y-section, with a vertical column in the new underground concourse. We had to introduce a double-stack circulatory system from the high-level DLR platform through the JLE platforms and down into the underground concourse. We proposed enclosing the high-level DLR platform in a monocoque shell to protect passengers from the bracing winds and driving rain that sweeps across the open site. That proposal had to be

abandoned because it was considered too expensive to build. We retained the sectional geometry using the stainless steel outriggers to hold an external glass screen in place. The outriggers were built but the glass screen was omitted following a value-engineering exercise.

To introduce natural daylight into the underground concourse, we formed a 25 m by 6 m opening in the JLE platform, framed by deep beams. WSP proved to the client that the upstands around the structural opening forming the track edge could resist the impact of train derailment. Our civil engineering partners then detailed the structure to be precast in segments weighing no more than 34 tonnes, so that they could be

glazed canopy to escalators

platform view

transported by rail from Tarmac's precast yard in Stamford, to Canning Town. It was a phenomenal exercise and a clever piece of construction engineering using sliding techniques, hydraulic jacks and push launch. The Y-shaped columns were lifted off the train bogeys and landed on their preformed bases using the shortest-ever tower cranes. Once all the splayed columns were in position and the cross bracing beams section was connected, a temporary sliding scaffold was erected to push launch the platform and track structural segments into place in 12 m lengths. The post-tensioned DLR platform was made up of transverse diaphragm units linked by short segmental box sections.

Glued segmental construction allowed the boxes to be placed and interconnected without the need for cranage.

We chose three durable materials for the surface finish to the structure – aluminium, stainless steel and concrete. We were concerned about the long stretches of fair-faced concrete walls separating the bus station from the railway lines and other areas. They needed lifting visually. We proposed tiling the walls in bright yellow, but it was not carried out due to cost. The vertically integrated JLE and DLR structure was sufficiently interesting sculpturally to remain monochromatic. We were pleased that most of the

detailed seating, lighting and signage that we designed was incorporated on the station. Roland Paoletti encouraged each of the architectural teams to design such components, as they might be adopted and standardised as line-wide elements for all the platforms.

The lower concourse was lined with curved, anodised-aluminium panels with flush rivets inspired by the early tube trains that were so elegantly streamlined in aluminium. The aluminium scoops light into the concourse and onto the platforms beneath the long concrete cantilevers. The bus station takes this concept a stage further, incorporating a wide, central, glazed

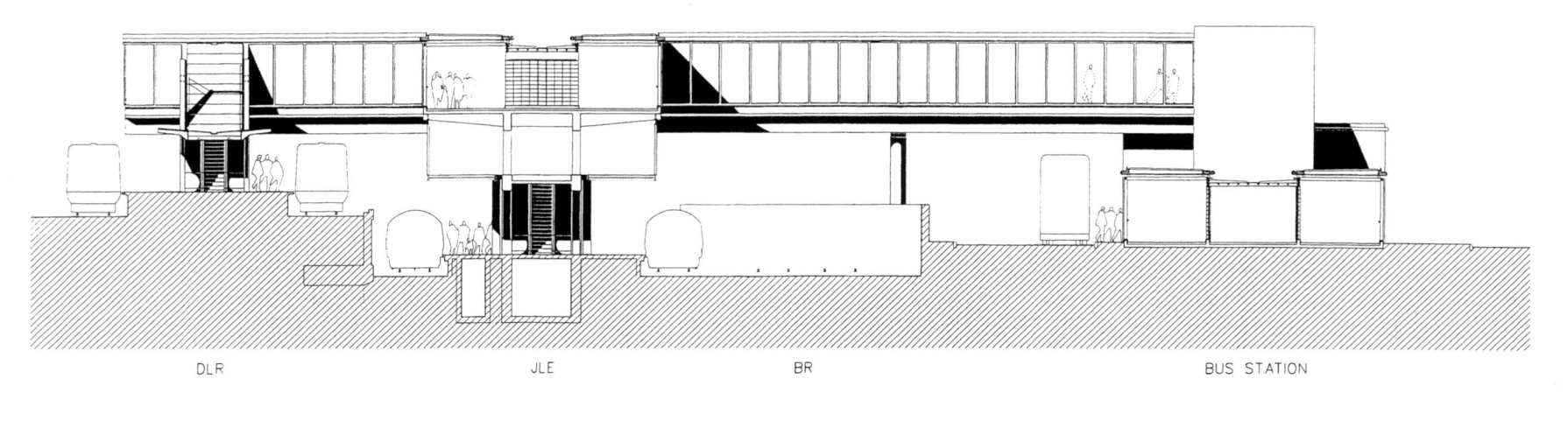

DLR JLE BR BUS STATION

design development:
elevation of option for
overhead bridge link

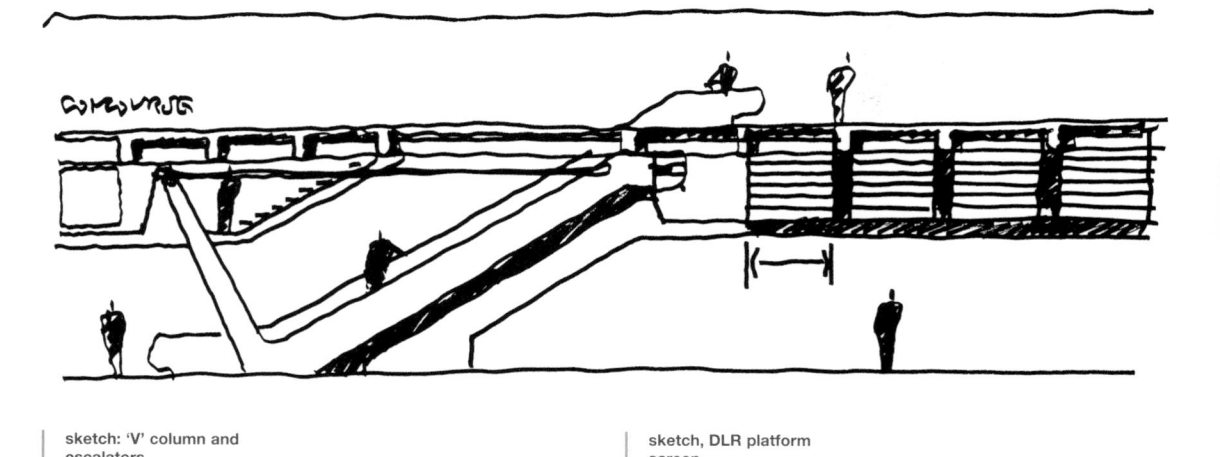

sketch: 'V' column and
escalators

sketch, DLR platform
screen

area between the roof canopy, which brings light into the concourse below. An important piece of history is commemorated on the walls of the bus station leading down to the lower concourse level. An iron plate that was part of the hull of the warship *HMS Warrior* (which was built in Canning Town in 1860) marks the site of the Thames Iron Works, one of the greatest ship–building companies in the late nineteenth century.

We have often been asked about the process leading to the completion of this complex structure. If there was a frustration it was in not being employed by the JLE to monitor the job on site through to its completion. When

We were pleased that most of the detailed seating, lighting and signage that we designed was incorporated on the station. Roland Paoletti encouraged each of the architectural teams to design such components.

longitudinal section: JLE
ground level, DLR roof level

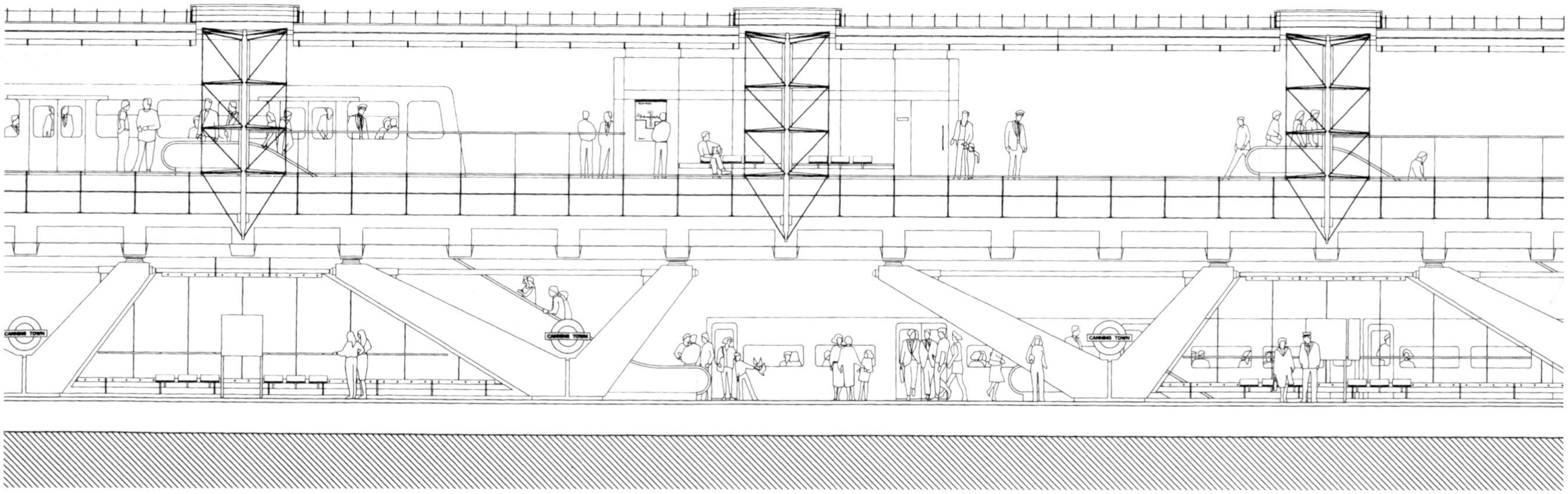

An important piece of history is commemorated on the walls of the bus station leading down to the lower concourse level. An iron plate that was part of the hull of the warship *HMS Warrior* (which was built in Canning Town in 1860) marks the site of the Thames Iron Works, one of the greatest ship-building companies in the late nineteenth century.

we had completed the design and the work had been tendered, the JLE Project Architects then took a more active role in the day-to-day detailing and administration of the work, until they handed over responsibility to the JLE Engineers, who supervised the construction. We had no presence on the site. If a piece of concrete was poorly cast it was the JLE Engineers who would decide if it should be recast. Invariably it was not done. When you look at Canary Wharf Station, for example, you see in situ concrete with a fine finish. In our view it should not have cost significantly more to have achieved a similar surface finish at Canning Town. Stations are built to last a long time, which makes it even more important to achieve a high-quality finish.

Overall the station is still a significant structure. It has been an achievement to have guided the design through the minefield of bureaucracy and, at times, opposition to our ideas. The LUL design manuals were devised primarily for underground stations, not surface structures and it was a struggle to obtain approval for ideas that did not strictly conform to an accepted way of designing a station. Although the process was exceptionally challenging, in the end the result demonstrates that anything is possible given persistence and commitment on the part of a team with a common aim.

Civil Engineer: WSP
Main Contractor: John Mowlem Construction

ten

◎ **West Ham** Architect: van Heyningen and Haward Architects

Birkin Haward, van Heyningen and Haward Architects

When the client invited architects to design the three above-ground stations at the end of the Jubilee Line, it had been decided that the civil engineers should be the lead consultants and the architects would be their sub-contractors. This is the reverse of the policy that was adopted for the below-ground stations, and it is surprising when you think of the magnitude of civil engineering involved in those undertakings. Our contracts were the last to be let, and we had the impression they were funded from the small change left over from the other projects.

Hammersmith & City
and District lines

Main line trains ≷

platform view

Our choice of architecture was not high-tech, nor a lightweight glass and steel affair, but robust
and contextural using brickwork, stainless steel, timber and glass blocks with enduring brass
treads for the stairways, durable concrete for the frame and stove-enamelled signage.

sketch: entrance
perspective

sketch: entrance
elevation

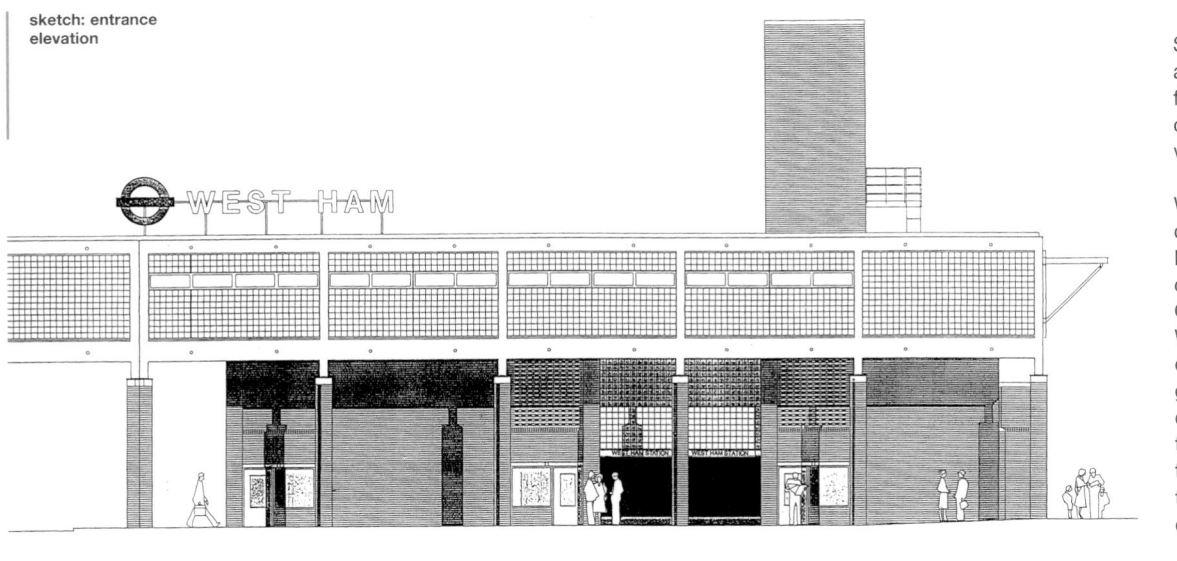

Six civil engineering consultants together with architectural practices – of whom we were one – pitched for the job of designing West Ham. The civil engineering consultants were appointed first and they had to choose which architect to run with. We teamed up with WSP.

We confess to being influenced by the 1930s' station designs of Holden on the Piccadilly and Metropolitan Lines, and were particularly impressed with the lofty ceiling, cheery brightness and refreshing modernism of Oakwood, which we regard as a poor man's Canary Wharf. There was not much time to develop our ideas as our appointment was made very late in the day. We were given the job in June1991 and had to have our tender drawings finalised by the end of the year. In the limited time that we had available, we attempted to use a mix of traditional and modern materials that would withstand the wear and tear of the public contact areas. Our choice of architecture was not high-tech, nor a

station entrance

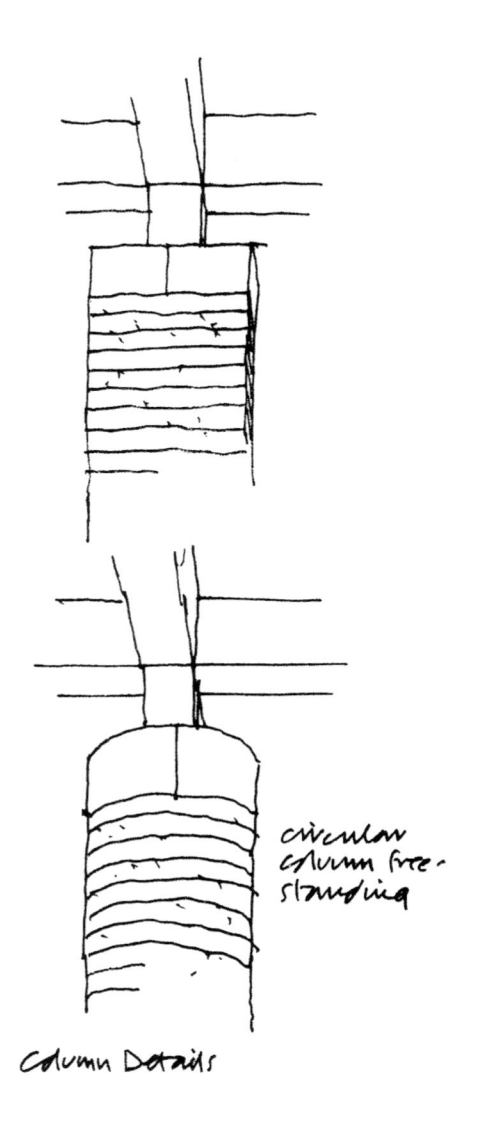

circular
column free-
standing

Column Details

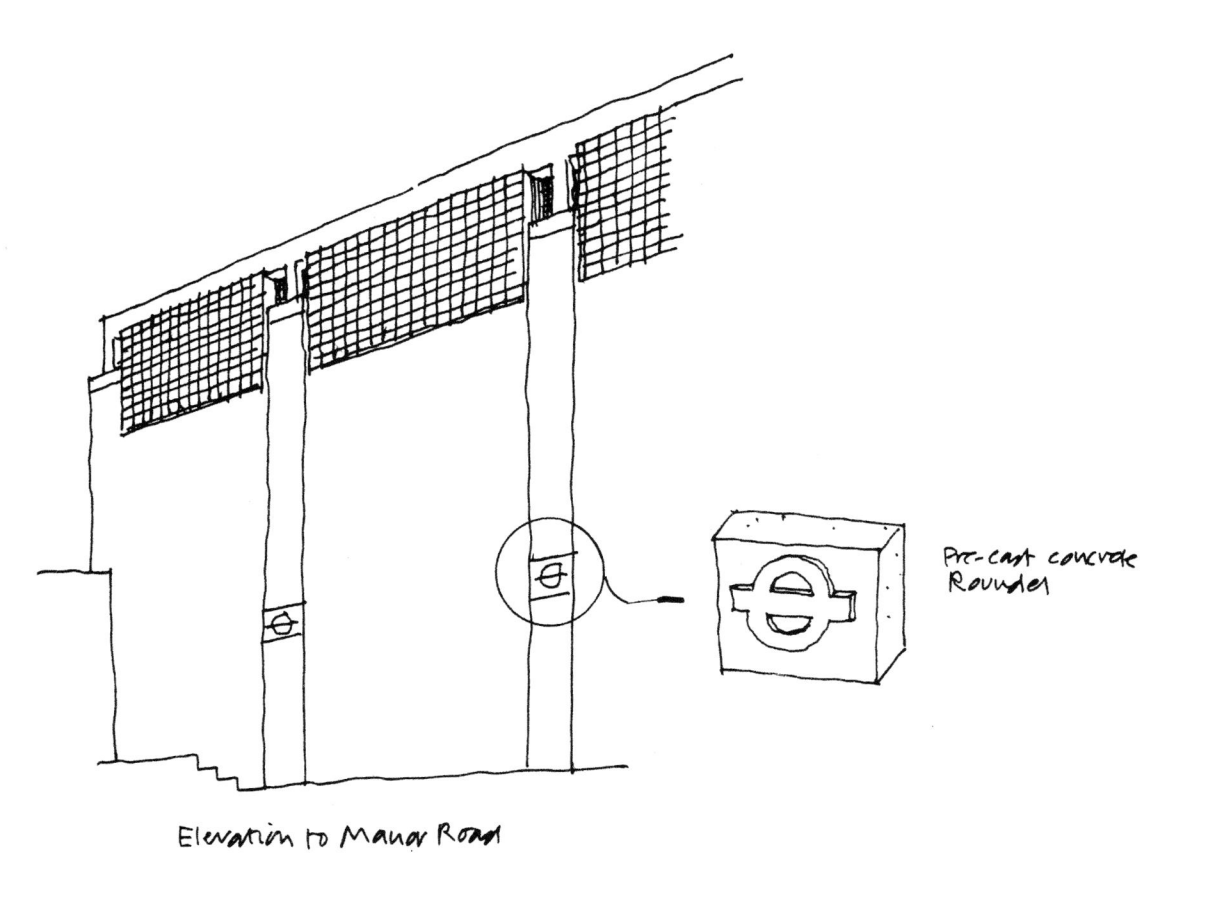

Elevation to Manor Road

Pre-cast concrete
Rounder

The concrete columns are encased in Ibstock Red brickwork to give additional strength and an attractive appearance.

lightweight glass and steel affair, but robust and contextural using brickwork, stainless steel, timber and glass blocks with enduring brass treads for the stairways, durable concrete for the frame and stove-enamelled signage. We had problems trying to reconcile the services provision in our scheme as we had limited help from the JLE services team during the design period. In the end we decided to contain the services in horizontal ducts attached like panniers to the underside of the building. It turned out to be a very good solution.

West Ham is primarily an interchange enabling passengers to move between the District and Metropolitan Lines, the North London Line and the JLE. There was an existing ticket hall that served the District and Metropolitan Lines and North London Line, which we had to have rebuilt. In summary the new station

consists of five principal elements – refurbishing the existing ticket hall, building the new ticket hall, creating a bridge link across Manor Road to the new platforms and building the new platforms for the JLE and North London Line. The new ticket hall has been designed as a welcoming, arcaded entrance that addresses a small formal square opposite the shops on Memorial Avenue. The new bridge link across Manor Road we felt should become part of the new ticket hall and an integral part of the public face of the new station complex. The overall composition and the choice of a brick facade is largely a response to the residential character of the neighbouring buildings.

The desire for an elegant structural solution has been paramount particularly in the flexibility and adaptability of the design for future installations and maintenance of

Our overall budget of
£10 million for construction
was modest compared with
the £360 million given to
Canary Wharf.

services. Slots built into the structure permit service
runs to reach all the parts of the station in an organised
fashion. The design task was to develop an integrated
structure on a modular grid, which could extend over
the whole station and yet respond to the conditions
imposed by each of the five building elements. The 6 m
by 6 m modular grid of the structural system responded
well to these criteria, with the superstructure defined by
post and beam construction, featuring 275 mm by
275 mm concrete columns. The concrete columns are
encased in Ibstock Red brickwork to give additional
strength and an attractive appearance. Where the
columns are freestanding as they are on the platforms,
they are circular. Extensive use of glass blocks has been
introduced across the bridge link and above the roofline.
Besides increasing the transparency of the public areas
by day, glass was particularly important in the
perception of the station at night as a beacon providing

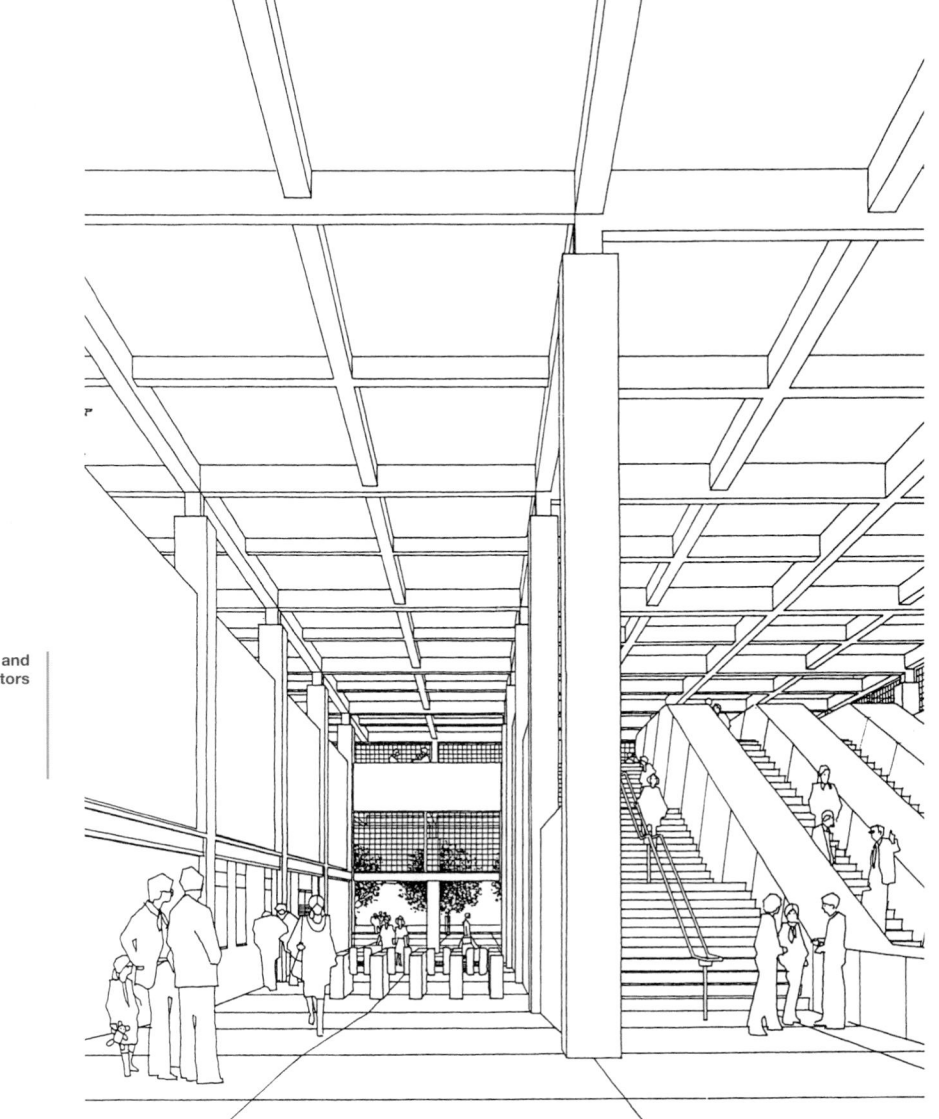

sketch: ticket hall and
escalators

glass block wall link bridge

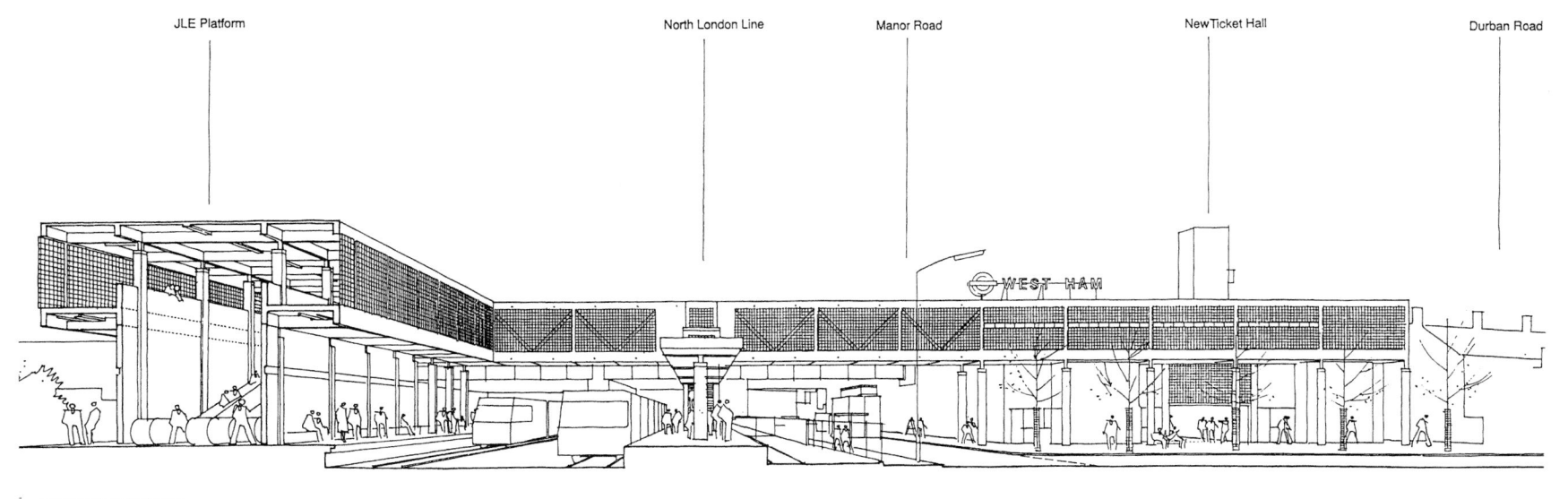

JLE Platform North London Line Manor Road NewTicket Hall Durban Road

**schematic: platforms
and link bridge**

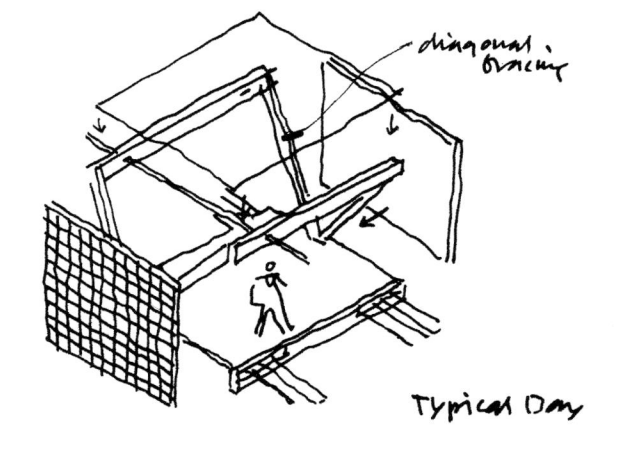

Besides increasing the
transparency of the public
areas by day, glass was
particularly important in the
perception of the station at
night as a beacon providing an
open, safe area for access.

an open, safe area for access. The glass blocks are
durable and self cleansing, which is important as we had
noticed that virtually no cleaning is done on a regular
basis in the existing underground stations.

Roland Paoletti was very supportive throughout the
whole process and when we presented our sketch ideas
to him and his team we got their full backing. Our overall
budget of £10 million for construction was modest
compared with the £360 million given to Canary Wharf.
Yes, we could have and should have asked for a little bit
more funding on reflection. We delivered over 700
working drawings to the client folded neatly into
numerous boxes, on completion of our design contract.

The finished building would have looked better and more
unified had we been asked to supervise the construction.
The client did not want us to participate, suggesting
perhaps that we would have been too critical of the
contractor's work and demand higher standards of
workmanship, which might have increased the cost. We
are not happy about many aspects of the built scheme –
particularly the concrete surface finish for example – it is
covered in blowholes and blemishes and badly finished.
We feel it would not have cost a great deal more to have
this aspect of the work properly supervised.

Civil Engineer: WSP
Contractor: Mowlem

eleven

◎ **Stratford platforms and accommodation building**
Architect: Troughton McAslan
Piers Smerin, Eldridge Smerin Architects, (formerly Troughton McAslan)

The scope and brief was to design three covered platforms that formed the eastern end of the Jubilee Line termination, together with accommodation for train staff, track maintenance personnel, and various power supply and signalling equipment rooms for the line. From the start the project appeared to be of lesser importance to LUL than the other stations and was to be subsumed within an overall redevelopment of the station concourse that both LUL and British Rail were wrestling for control of. In the end the design commission was awarded to Troughton McAslan as an add-on to their commission for Canning Town interchange to the south.

seating pod

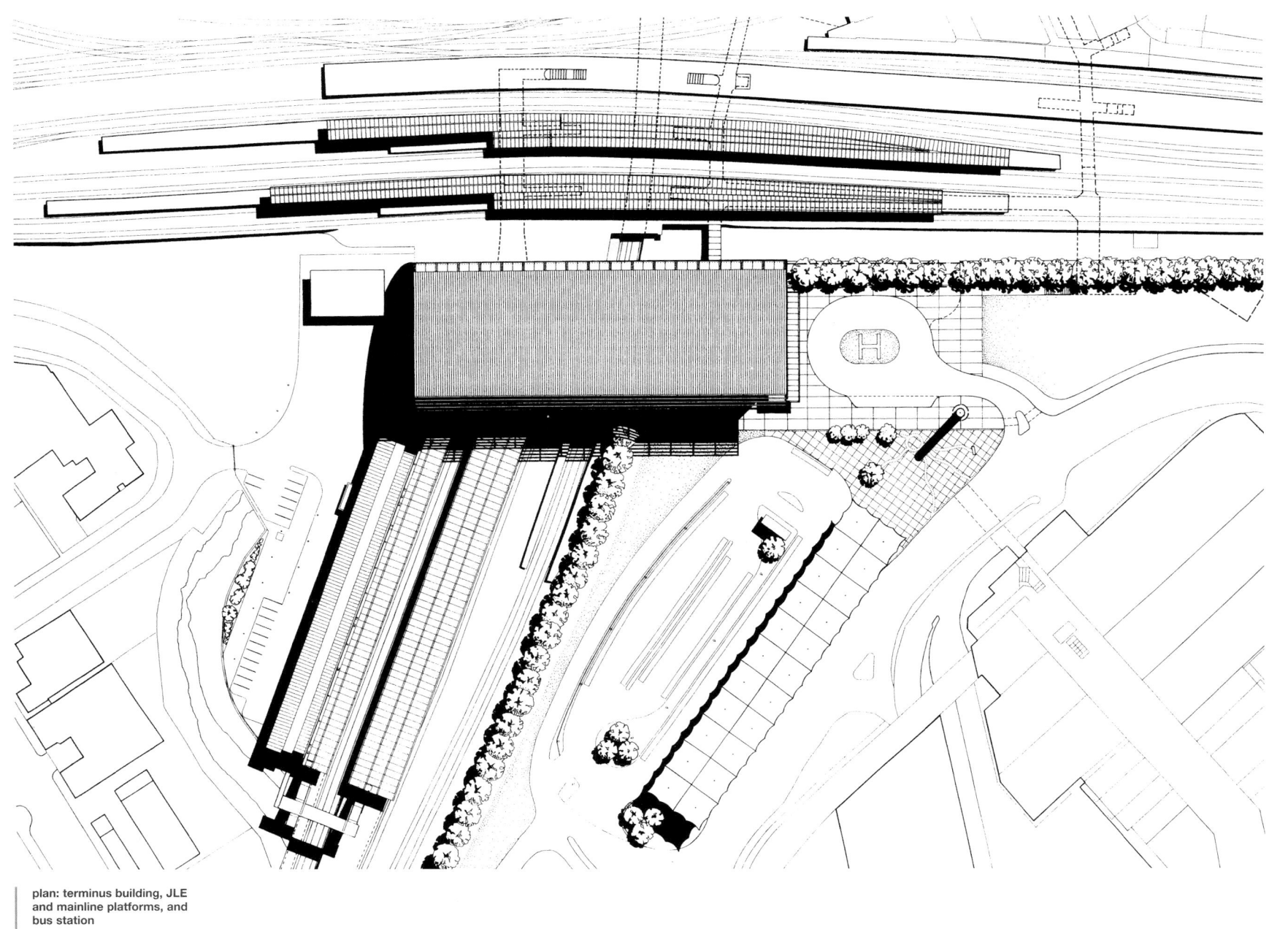

**plan: terminus building, JLE
and mainline platforms, and
bus station**

The position and arrangement
of the tracks was given. The
location of the other facilities,
however, offered possibilities.

In contrast to this attitude of dismissing Stratford Station
as of peripheral importance, located as it was on the
eastern fringe of London, our preference was to regard it
as an opportunity to celebrate the new line in a modest
way. After all it was the gateway for the Stratford area to
the revitalised docklands and the emerging cultural
quarter of the capital around Southwark and
Bermondsey. It also offered the chance to create some
decent facilities for the Underground staff manning and
maintaining the line, to which little consideration
appeared to have been given, although we were mindful
that it would need some careful organisation to avoid
conflicting with the needs of the public realm of the
platforms.

The position and arrangement of the tracks was given.
The location of the other facilities, however, offered
possibilities. Early attempts to make the personnel and
equipment accommodation building bridge the tracks,
literally forming a gateway structure to the new line,
were defeated by the rapidly increasing amount of
spaces needed to house everyone in the building.
Almost by default the accommodation block became a
building stretching for over 100 m, along most of the
length of the platforms, on vacant land to the north. The
evolving nature of the brief demanded a clear building
strategy to avoid it becoming a chaotic array of spaces
and doorways like so much traditional trackside
accommodation. We introduced a two-storey-high

central platform canopy

screen wall to shield the actual areas of accommodation from the public world of the platforms beyond, which had a controlled series of entrances to give access to the individual areas of the building on two levels. Each of the three entrances and their adjacent stairway would be dedicated to train crew, permanent way personnel or equipment maintenance staff and their respective sets of accommodation.

The accommodation building is a fair-faced concrete frame structure with ceramic-faced, external, infill blockwork panels up to first floor level and sand blasted, stack bonded, internal blockwork partition walls. The base of the building at track level contains all the

equipment rooms. The blockwork construction allowed the sizes and numbers of rooms to be easily varied during the design development phase and also allowed areas of louvres, ductwork and other openings to be built in as needed. The high degree of flexibility this afforded LUL was fully exploited during the design process and early construction phase, with room configurations going through numerous iterations. Above ground floor sits the inhabited areas with showers, toilets, changing areas, recreation spaces and booking areas for the train and permanent way crews who use the building on a 24-hour cycle. To raise the quality of these spaces a high vaulted roof with clerestory glazing was added with a continuous strip of glazed windows giving daylight to the central

recreation and office spaces. Externally, the upper floor is swathed in honed, grey-limestone panels, which are very concrete in colour, that help assert its importance as staff space over the variegated grid of the technical spaces below. Although the staff spaces on the upper level were intended to be day-lit and naturally ventilated, perversely because it was LUL property, they insisted that their normal design standards were applied with the building sealed and mechanically serviced as if it were 20 m below ground!

The screen wall dividing the building from the platforms was intended to be clad in patinated copper panels giving a rich yet natural quality to what is an abstract

accommodation building

← Platform 14

Patinated zinc was used giving the screen wall a rather more serious and reticent air although the crisply folded detailing of the zinc with its flush jointed surface is very much to the scheme's benefit.

It also offered the chance to create some decent facilities for the Underground staff manning and maintaining the line, to which little consideration appeared to have been given, although we were mindful that it would need some careful organisation to avoid conflicting with the needs of the public realm of the platforms.

surface of huge proportions. Regrettably this was vetoed by British Rail's architects who felt it would compete with their design for the new concourse. Instead, patinated zinc was used giving the screen wall a rather more serious and reticent air although the crisply folded detailing of the zinc with its flush jointed surface is very much to the scheme's benefit.

The platforms themselves were intentionally kept as simple, calm, orderly spaces with an expansive feel. A regular grid of columns supports a series of cantilever arms all formed from rolled steelwork sections with discrete, flush, bolted connections, which support smooth, metal-clad canopy wings covering each platform. The wider central platform canopy section has

rows of white-rendered, soffit panels running down the middle to brighten the ceiling. The platforms house a series of ceramic-faced blockwork fins with integral stainless steel seats and other elements of platform furniture. The zinc-clad screen wall of the building forms a backdrop to the activity of the platforms.

A request by LUL late in the design process, to provide a pedestrian bridge linking the three platforms, was met by building a further zinc-clad fin wall to match the height of the building on each platform. These are notched back to support a steel framed box beam that forms the bridge deck and roof; the bridge is accessed by in situ concrete stairs. Although the original fine mesh infill panels to the bridge sides have been replaced with

heavier perforated metal panels, the sculptural qualities of the bridge as a whole make it a satisfying 'gateway' structure to the new line.

The pedestrian bridge also forms a fine vantage point to take in the elements of the JLE station, the new terminus concourse and the bus station opposite, which have combined to give Stratford a transport interchange that is of the highest quality. Like the rest of the JLE stations it hopes to make underground travel pleasurable, if only momentarily.

Civil Engineer: WSP
Contractor:　John Mowlem

link bridge to accommodation building

twelve

◎ Stratford terminus and interchange

Architect: Wilkinson Eyre Architects Ltd
Jim Eyre, Wilkinson Eyre Architects Ltd

The new terminus building, which runs parallel to the brick arched embankment of the Central Line and mainline tracks and platforms was designed facing the town. In the competition brief it was shown overlooking the mainline high-level platforms. The brief was reinterpreted to take account of its urban context, its prominent location, the public perception of such a building and the fact that it was the terminus of the Jubilee Line. We won the competition with that argument.

perspective from end
elevation

end elevation

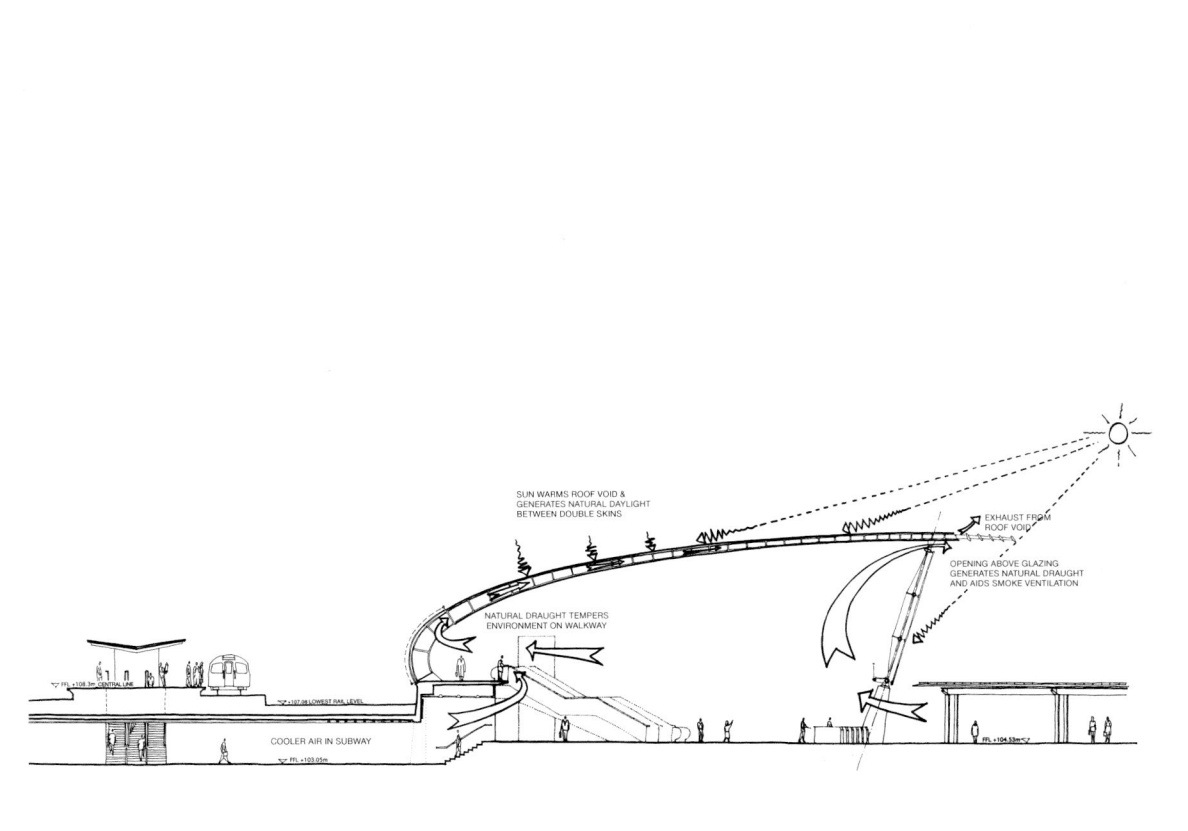

SUN WARMS ROOF VOID &
GENERATES NATURAL DAYLIGHT
BETWEEN DOUBLE SKINS

EXHAUST FROM
ROOF VOID

OPENING ABOVE GLAZING
GENERATES NATURAL DRAUGHT
AND AIDS SMOKE VENTILATION

NATURAL DRAUGHT TEMPERS
ENVIRONMENT ON WALKWAY

FFL +108.3m CENTRAL LINE

+107.08 LOWEST RAIL LEVEL

COOLER AIR IN SUBWAY

FFL +103.05m

FFL +104.53m

The whole of the roof void is used as a thermal flue drawing air across the concourse and provides a passive ventilation system. The smooth uninterrupted roof soffit acts as a reflector for artificial light, bouncing it back to illuminate the floor.

Making the connections to the other transport hubs was complex because the entrance to the terminus was on the east, which means pedestrians have to use a very long subway to get to the mainline platforms. Thrust boring was used to create access subways under the embankment of the high-level tracks and platforms – it was a solution that came with the brief.

The architectural concept evolved around the decision to develop a roof structure and concourse with a public face that looks outwards rather than inwards, while endeavouring to resolve the circulation puzzle and ease interchange between several train services. The primary components of the project were first to design an interchange concourse on two levels traversing the North London Line – which runs north–south at ground level – and second, to thrust bore subways under the existing high-level platforms that run east–west, which will facilitate direct interchange with the Jubilee Line. In

addition to the interchange complexities, the project design also had to accommodate construction in two phases: the first to allow for the JLE platforms and a second to provide a ticket hall with direct street access replacing the previous obscure and convoluted arrangements. Although the design did take phasing into account, in the end the construction of the whole station was carried out in a single entity, as funding for the entire project became available prior to the commencement of work on site in April 1996.

The form of the building is expressed as a curved roof springing from an upper level walkway, geometrically defined as a sector of an ellipse in section. The apparently simple form of the building serves a number of separate functions – it shows a dramatic public face to the town, and, being south facing, the shaded glazing produces good quality light. The whole of the roof void is used as a thermal flue drawing air across the lightweight truss supporting the glass wall

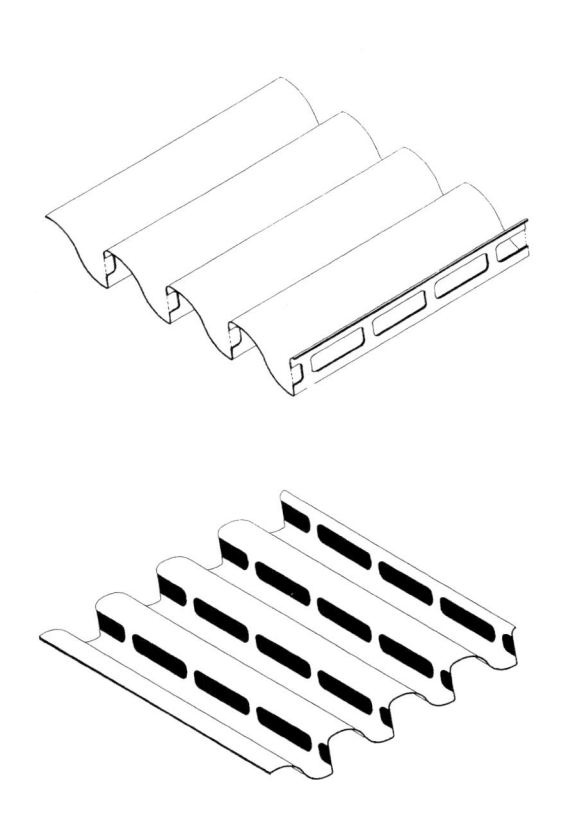

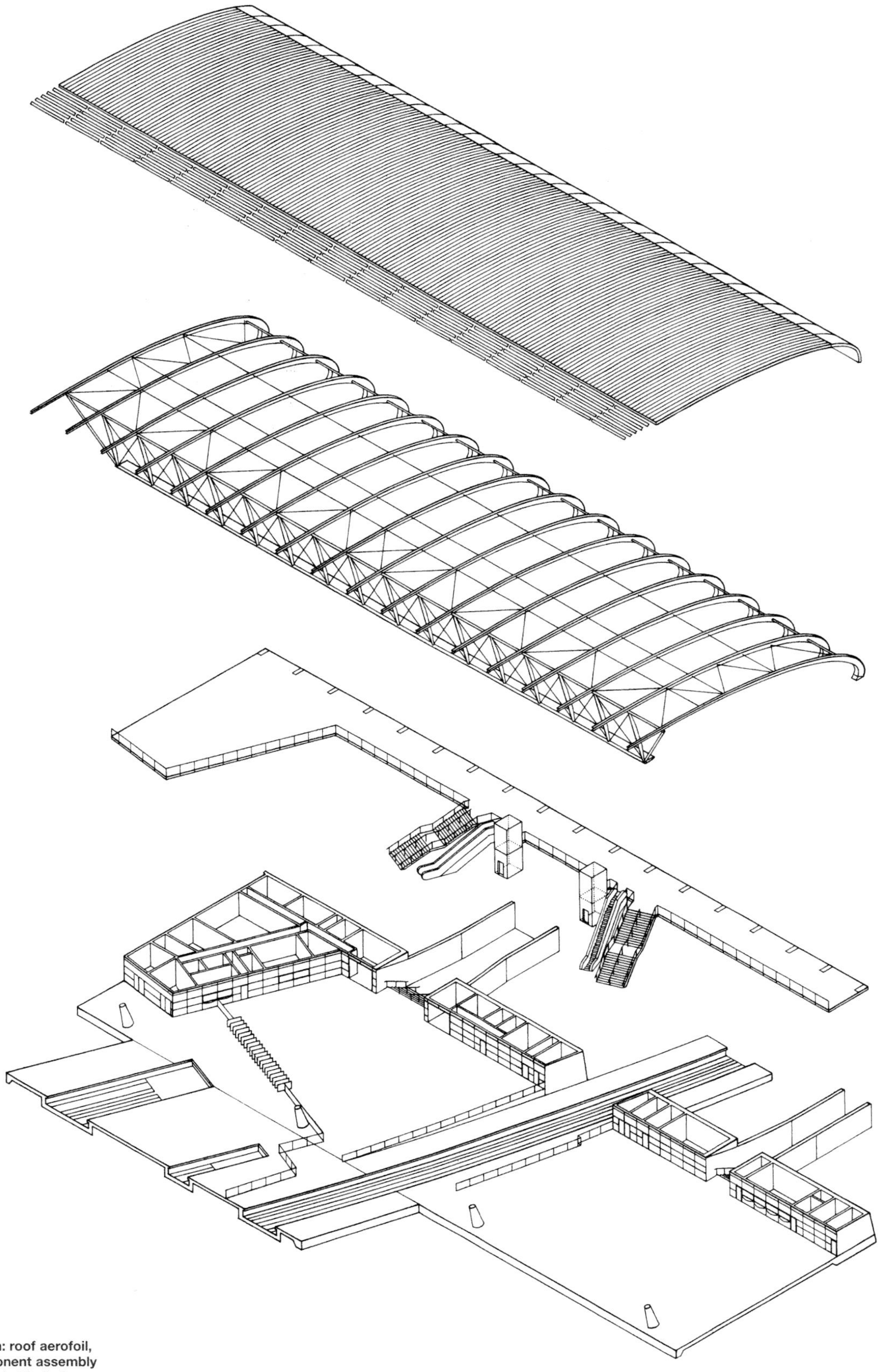

concourse and provides a passive ventilation system. The smooth uninterrupted roof soffit acts as a reflector for artificial light, bouncing it back to illuminate the floor. The ceiling is lined with purpose-made ribbed aluminium extrusions that have been perforated to be acoustically absorbent. The uplighting of the ceiling, which is free of suspended fittings or equipment, lends an ethereal quality to the space, both internally and externally.

The front truss of the glazed south elevation is inclined at 11° to the vertical, which adds a visual dynamic to the space. The truss, which is 8 m deep, spans three bays, each measuring 30 m. One bay spans the end of the Jubilee Line platforms, a second bay spans the North London Line and the third defines the entrance. The bottom boom of the truss, which is also a maintenance walkway for the glass screen, sits on cast metal joints that have been bolted into the tops of three large

sketch: roof aerofoil, component assembly and ticket hall plan

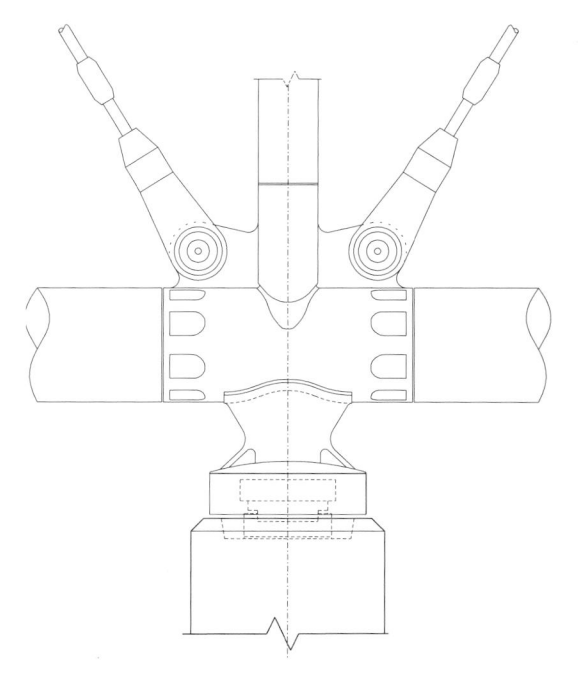

detail: steelwork node
and column joint

The front truss of the glazed south elevation is inclined at 11° to the vertical, which adds a visual dynamic to the space. The truss, which is 8 m deep, spans three bays, each measuring 30 m.

tapering precast concrete shell columns. A beam attached to the bottom truss member supports the up-lighters illuminating the canopy soffit and other station equipment. Glazing is supported by vertical spider cable trusses with bolted connections through to the glass panels. This glass filigree structure of very lightweight members acts as a counterpoint to the smooth uninterrupted curvature of the concourse soffit.

Tapering steel plate girder ribs, mostly hidden within the smooth roof covering, are visible on the north side of the building, over the curved glass facade that faces the zone reserved for the controversial CrossRail Project, and which look out towards the high-level platforms. Fritting to the glass provides shade for commuters crossing the North London Line via the high-level walkway inside. The cantilever ribs reach out from the

high-level walkway to support and shape the entire concourse roof. Each rib is supported on a giant casting that is bolted down using high-strength macalloy bars. The tips of the cantilever ribs are propped by the deep truss, which frames the glazed south elevation window. The stainless steel linings to partitions, ticket hall fascia and barriers have been 'shot peened' to give the surface a stippled fine texture. Using a plain polished steel

glazed south elevation, column support and bottom boom

**sketch: vertical glazing
truss and bottom boom**

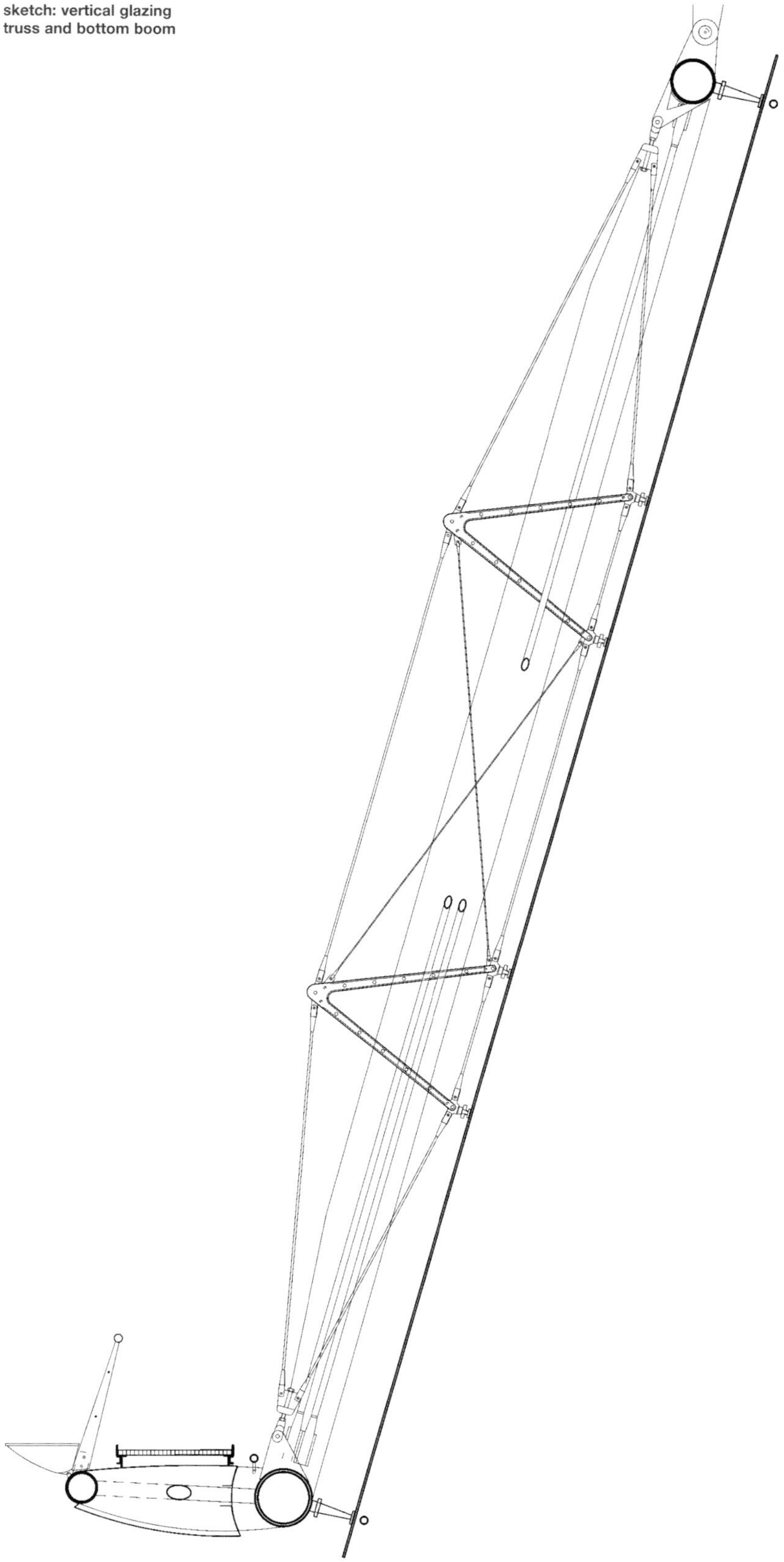

surface shows up every mark and thumb print. The floor is tiled with terrazzo, the subways are lined with vitreous-enamelled steel sheeting. Improvements to the access, signage and routing from the grubby high-level platforms and buildings that serve the mainline and Central Line network, were carried out, but do not look much different after such cosmetic facelifts.

The station forecourt forms a plaza that links the bus station and vehicle set-down areas with the commercial centre of Stratford. At night the station glows in the townscape, providing a bright welcoming aspect.

Civil Engineer: Ove Arup
Contractor: Kvaerner Construction

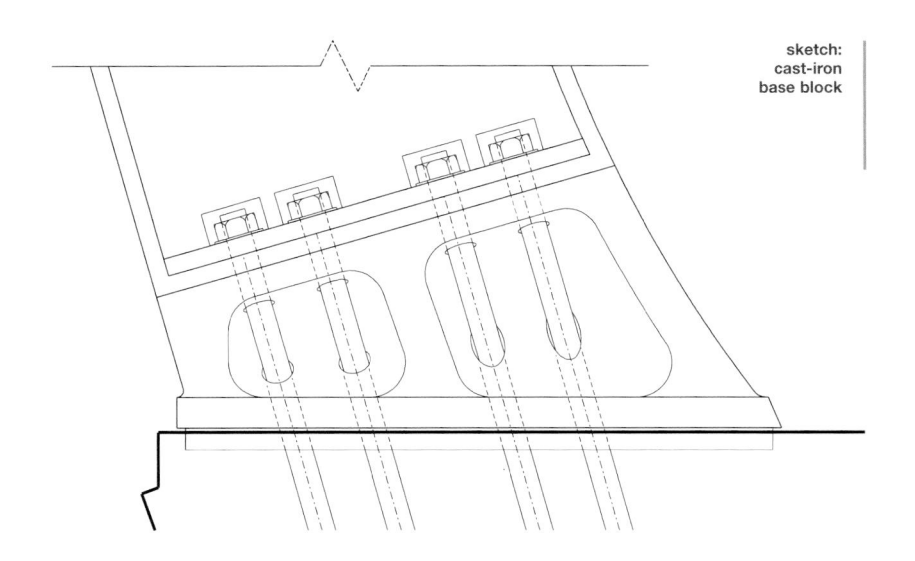

sketch:
cast-iron
base block

Glazing is supported by vertical spider cable trusses with bolted connections through to the glass panels. This glass filigree structure of very lightweight members acts as a counterpoint to the smooth uninterrupted curvature of the concourse soffit.

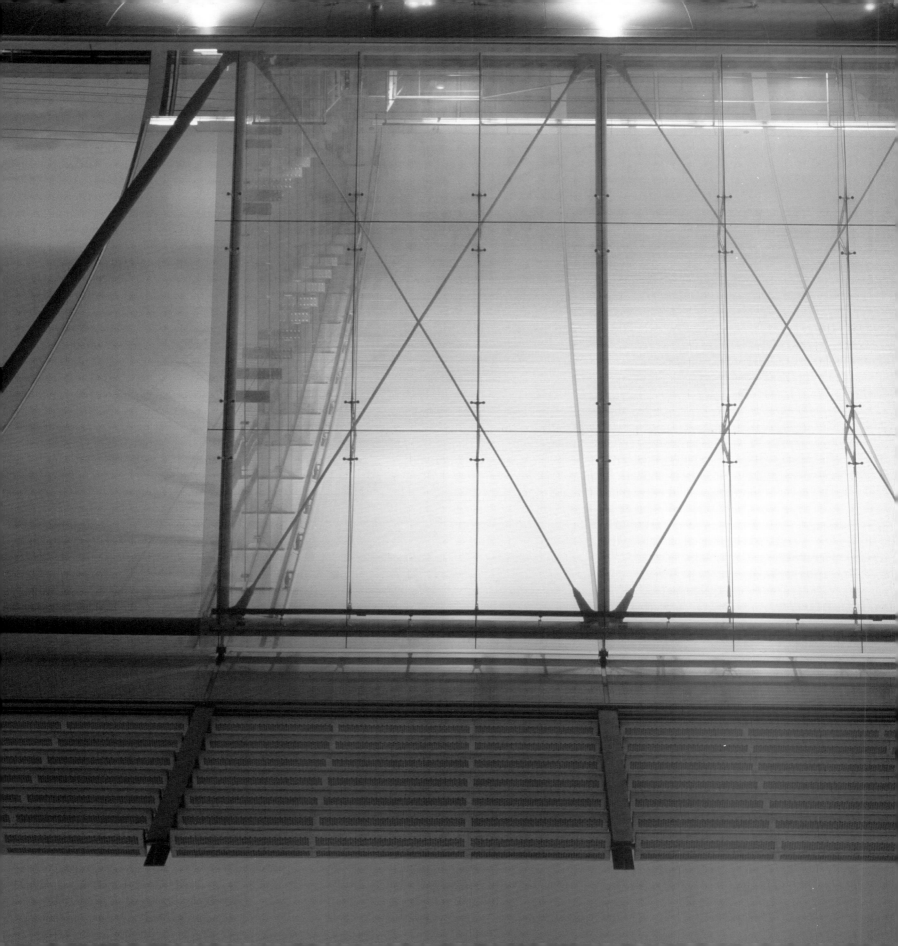

© **First impressions**   Mike Foley, retired bank manager and poet

Stratford terminus. Here beauty is not sacrificed for structure. I like the idea that the roof is used to change the air. It is a comfortable space and I am happy to linger beneath this beautiful curving canopy and admire the glass balustrade to the staircase and walkways.

West Ham I find oppressive and overbearing. There is a lack of light in the ticket hall corridors and too much red brick everywhere. I find that surprising for such a modern station.

Canning Town is stupendous because of its creative use of concrete and the fact that there is no adornment – function and aesthetic merged into one. There is so much natural light flooding into the station passageways and ticket hall. There is the drama of the light rail passing overhead and the clean lines of the metal canopy to the platforms and the bus station. The experience is expansive and liberating.

North Greenwich. I am having difficulty making my mind up about this station. I find the blue restful and the ambience gives the impression of being in a cinema. But the colour is too dark and foreboding in many ways for safe usage. The silver vanes of the fire escape stairs are in sharp contrast with the dark background, which I only saw by chance when I was on the platform. I do not like the unfinished roof detail. Coming out of the station you see the wonderful glass-clad Foster bus station and frankly you do not want to go back underground but stay awhile to enjoy this graceful structure.

Canary Wharf. It is a cathedral of light and a vast ocean of space, order and intelligence. The ribbed concrete roof and external glass canopy at the exits are works of structural art that delight the senses and provide a focus and dynamic to the whole station. This is a statement about modern architecture as powerful as Wren's St Paul's Cathedral or Brunel's Paddington Station were in past centuries. It has opened my mind to the beauty of structural form – seeing the moulded concrete roof, and how the use of pure materials gives context and depth – stainless steel, glass and plain concrete. The massive elliptical columns rising up to the roof are so impressive and I am mesmerised by the magnificent dome of glass at the exits, where torrents of light pour down the escalator like a waterfall.

Canada Water. The most impressive part of it is visible above ground – the luminous glass rotunda and the fabulous bus station roof. The rotunda allows pools of light to pour into the lower parts of the station and is very reminiscent of the stations on the Piccadilly Line, particularly Oakwood. The need to build below an existing railway line constricted the station box and I find the lower half of it to be visually unimpressive. Looking down from the high walkway towards the platforms, I find the ceiling lacks finish and is covered with what looks like pieces of meccano. The station surface is covered in mosaic tiles which are altogether far too grey, and make the internal areas look featureless.

Bermondsey. I find this inspirational for a partially submerged station, particularly the pleasing blue of the continuous seating along the platform, seen on emerging from the train. Here function and art are combined in the concrete trusses bracing the walls. At ground level light poured through from every angle of the external surface. The artificial lighting is so subtle that it appears to be natural.

London Bridge. I am struck by the stove-enamelled panels on the access and platform tunnel walls and the free flowing use of space, despite being in tunnels – the cast-iron linings are an attractive feature of the station. Colour is used to distinguish the Northern Line from the Jubilee Line. The ceiling of the Borough High Street exit is beautiful, it has what I can only describe as the profile of upturned canoes, and in combination with the lighting it creates a wonderful visual effect. The original brick vaulted arches blend well with the modern section of the station, the vaulted ceiling of which is covered with terracotta tiles. But the brick stanchions of the old arches are encased in heavy concrete at floor level, which is out of all proportion and looks ugly and unsightly. Apart from this one blemish I am very impressed with this station.

Southwark. I like this station very much. The smooth, polished concrete block walls resemble marble and there is a feeling of spaciousness with good lighting. There is a lovely combination of brushed steel, aluminium and concrete. On climbing the escalator I was faced with a dome of blue glass, and as I went towards the exit barrier I moved from one circular light-filled roof space to another. It is a very uplifting experience.

Waterloo. Overall greyness, there seems no relief from this drab colour. The travelator is particularly depressing, with the total greyness of the surfaces. But the station itself is quite spacious, and areas within it flow freely from one to another.

Westminster. By far the most dramatic station of the JLE. This is not a station but an experience. It is a cavern of enormous proportion and scale. Structure and function are blended together to make a sort of organism whose energy is channelled and directed. The huge stresses of the enclosing walls are carried by massive columns and enormous bracing struts of tubular steel. Here function is everything and the drama of coping with stresses is played out before one's very eyes. It is like being on a film set.

Reflections – the opportunities taken and those that were lost

David Bennett, civil engineer

Having made several journeys along the JLE and looked at each station with a critical eye, there are aspects of the station architecture that continue to impress and others that disappoint. The architects appointed to work on the JLE station designs were asked to express the civil engineering of the construction with clarity and honesty, and to ensure the internal spaces catered for the anticipated passenger flows over the next half century. Adornment, frippery, mannerism and architectural vanity, often seen in building architecture, were to be kept under strict control. But in doing so did Roland Paoletti really believe that it was possible to muzzle certain architects who we all know like to dazzle and show off? Perhaps it was this dichotomy and diversity of architectural expression among the chosen ensemble that gave the JLE its verve and uniqueness and delivered what Paoletti was really hoping for. It certainly has succeeded – we are passionate about what we like and dislike about the new JLE stations and that is good.

The big statements – Canary Wharf, North Greenwich and Westminster – where most of the money was spent, as you might expect, never fail to impress, one way or another. Canary Wharf ranks highest in my estimation because the internal space is so well organised – the excess baggage and clutter of services and ticket counters are tucked neatly along the sides of the ticket hall. From platform level right up to the ticket hall you feel daylight filtering down and the vast airiness of an open corridor leading you skywards. The structure is pure, the clarity of the civil engineering faithful and the homogeneity of form lean in every detail. The concrete has not been covered in tiles, blockwork or aluminium panels but left exposed with the marks of its construction – the panel joint lines, and patina of hydration. The curved concrete openings, that support the glass canopy at the exits, have deep recess joints between the cast sections that beat out a vertical rhythm along its curvature. The upward lighting flooding the roof is as silvery as the sheen across a field of barley under a full moon. The station makes travel on the underground less stressful because on exiting you are left in a calm and peaceful disposition – the vastness of the ticket hall, the graceful lines of the roof rib sections, the smooth ovoid columns, the light dancing through the glass canopy – helping you forget the disruptions and overcrowding experienced during the train journey. By contrast, the more I see of it, the more of a disappointment and enigma North Greenwich becomes. The choice of deep-blue tiling is gloomy, the sombre darkness of the station is in contradiction with the brief. The power and creativity of the civil engineering is lost in the bulky shadows of the central walkway and dark walls, stifling the visibility and coherence of the internal space and access points to and from the platforms. It would have been sensational to have left the roof off, which is how this station was first conceived. When the decision was taken to enclose it, no attempt seems to have been made to rationalise the internal space to respond to this change. Westminster, on the other hand, is engineering theatre, the perfect backdrop for one of Wagner's great operas or the film set of the Titanic perhaps. It is a gigantic kinetic art show with escalators zigzagging their way up to ground level and ant-sized people moving about on them while a greenish-grey light washes over everything. The tubular steel struts bracing the diaphragm wall are like the branches of a tree that burst out of cylindrical trunks of concrete holding Portcullis House in place. For me the real excitement is looking for the outline of fossils imprinted on the diaphragm wall – frescos of the earth's geology – or the shadows playing on the texture and profile of the muscular bush-hammered grillage beams, and the varying sheen of light playing on the tubular steel struts that pin everything back. It is a pity the escalator housings are so bulky because they obstruct the visibility of the station shaft. I am told that the architects tried hard to reduce their bulk, but London Underground insisted on having covered access corridors under every one of them to allow an engineer to carry out inspections and maintenance without being seen.

When commenting on stations it is appropriate to group them together by their mode of construction. The cut-and-cover stations (where a large excavation is dug, the retaining walls are cast, the platform, ticket hall and escalators then sleeved into the cut before the roof is put over it) are Bermondsey, Canada Water, Canary Wharf, North Greenwich and Southwark. Comments on North Greenwich and Canary Wharf have already been made, so what about the other three? By far the most pleasing station of its type is Bermondsey. It is a jewel among all the underground stations, and should be the template for the design of all cut-and-cover stations on the network. The architects have understood and deliberately expressed the drama of both the temporary and

permanent civil engineering work, to give the station its form and interest. There is clarity in the articulation of internal space. Light entering the platform makes access and travel clear and easy – the concrete truss beams bracing the escalator shaft and retaining wall are powerful in scale yet delicate in their bone-china surface finish. The lightweight roof is well engineered; the structural elements contribute to the overall refinement of form – there is no artificiality or gimmicky glass panels or screens hiding the real structure. The neat, symmetrical underground emblem sitting on the roof of the station entrance and the blue continuous seating along the platform wall epitomise the character of this station for me – pure, simple and poetic. At the other end of the scale where decoration and mannerism intoxicate to excess is Southwark. There are many aspects of this station that are pleasing. The up-lighting in the concourse and escalator shafts is the best of all the smaller cut-and-cover boxes and tunnelled stations. The plain grey concrete tunnel lining in the platform enclosure, with the thin band of continuous white lighting running the length of the platform is warm, uncomplicated and calming. But the rest of the space is retrogressive and kitsch. Polished concrete blockwork masks the adits between the concourse and platforms,

and an absurd funnel of metal and glass obstructs the stairways leading to the escalator shafts. At the top of the escalator you are greeted by a curved wall of blue glass that is quite out of context for a civil engineering structure, no matter how beautiful it may be. It confuses, rather than encourages any sense of direction. The beams propping the opening to the roof above the glass wall are 'fashioned' into pretty curving sections. The rotunda in the ticket hall is a tribute to Holden and it does work well, but it is borrowed and dated and has nothing of the sleek modernity of Canada Water's fabulous glass rotunda. The canopy at Waterloo East Station on the other hand is superb, the elegance of its pure structural form and the modern twist to the station refurbishment works very well. One wonders why the architects did not have the courage to do the same in Southwark. Many of my friends think Southwark is a delight because they feel they are entering a building space not a station. The architects have indeed tried to make a building out of this station, blanking out the power of the base structure with adornment – for me that is sacrilege. By contrast Canada Water is honest and rugged; here structural form sculptures the spaces within it. It would have been better visually if the concrete walls were not covered in the 'flat'

colour of the grey mosaic tiles, in an attempt to simulate a concrete finish. The functional need for walkways, crossover links and a massive box structure slicing through to cradle the East London Line above the JLE tracks does clog the openness of the station once past the ticket barriers. Although the metal grillage to the concrete ceilings looks cheap and unfinished, the station appeals to me on two counts. It has a romantic link with Marc Brunel's Thames Tunnel if you use the East London Line, and it has the most perfect entrance rotunda of any station of the entire underground network. It ranks, in my opinion, with Charles Holden's 1930s Sudbury Station entrance. The transparency of the glass-clad entrance and the silvery reflection from the metal-clad roof act as beacons, welcoming and directing travellers and users towards it, especially at night. It helps that the JLE entrance links seamlessly with Eva Jericna's bus station canopy. The meticulous attention to the detail and layout of acoustic damping holes on the underside of the bus station canopy creates a beautiful repeating pattern across the entire surface – here functionality becomes a work of art. Your senses impel you to walk the length and breadth of the bus station canopy and to circle the rotunda one more time.

There are two tunnelled stations on the JLE at London Bridge and Waterloo. Both of them are transport interchanges and the most difficult stations to engineer and construct. London Bridge is a far more coherent and unifying collection of conduit spaces than Waterloo. From floor to head level deep-blue stove-enamelled panels cover the voids between the cast-iron tunnel-lining ribs. The panels graduate in colour to a light grey over the crown of the tunnel where they have slots cut into them for acoustic damping. The pattern and flow of the panel arrangement vividly emphasise the curvature, reticulation and construction of the tunnels, whilst not attempting to cover them up. The up-lighting of the main concourse as you step out of the platform tunnel is exceptional, and despite the bulk of the lighting booms overhead there is a feeling of brightness and spaciousness. For some reason, the graduation from deep blue to light grey panels was not repeated in the escalator shaft, where much of the tunnel linings above head height were left exposed and painted grey. Consequently it has created a gloomy ceiling with the overhead lighting boom unintentionally dominant. On the positive side the coffered precast shell roof at the Borough High Street exit is a delight, as are the original vaulted brick arch ceilings leading away from the mainline station

entrance. The only disappointment is the unsightly concrete boots cast around the base of the brick piers supporting the arches. Surely a more sensitive and less intrusive engineering solution could have been found? Waterloo has spacious tunnel corridors and good lighting, but it is a pity the drama of expressing the tunnel rib construction has been annulled by the monotonous grey of the panel colour. Why did the design team not follow the bold ideas developed for the London Bridge tunnels or put some art on the walls?

At the eastern end of the extension are the three above-ground stations culminating in the stunning glass-clad enclosure of Stratford terminus. A lot has been written about the Stratford terminus. For me the lightweight truss standing 8 m high and spanning the length of the building supported on four precast columns is a work of engineering art. So is the wonderful sweep of the silky smooth canopy roof and the crisply detailed connection of steelwork, holding down bolts and foundation plinth visible on the high-level walkway. I take time out whenever I can to have a coffee break here – it is such a luminous and liberating space to be in. The other above-ground stations are Canning Town and West Ham – the

chalk and cheese of the JLE. Canning Town is an engineering wonder, dynamic in concept yet with every imaginable obstruction to surmount – overhead power lines, a river on one side, a major roadway on the other. Its execution and construction deserve a book in its own right. There is much to admire throughout the structure – the smooth lines of the V-shaped columns striding along the platforms, their asymmetrical configuration giving the whole assembly momentum and rhythm. The sleek aerofoil canopy of the platform roof, the light filtering through into the underground concourse, the illuminated corridors leading to the ticket hall and towards the bus station, all give the building a unifying experience that contributes to the coherence of the architecture. For added drama there is the DLR station riding piggyback over the JLE platforms. West Ham is an oddity rather like North Greenwich. Some of the best concept drawings and detailed sketches were produced to explain the designs for West Ham. They were beautifully composed hand-made sketches. In the progression from black and white drawing to red brick realisation, the station buildings appear to be a throwback to 1930s underground architecture, and do not sit well with the modernity of the other JLE stations. The red, brick-clad

structure has made the station monumental and overbearing rather than open and expansive. In black and white, the brick-clad face looks more like stone and quite fantastic. The chunky glass-clad walkway over the road to the ticket hall is strangely confining as it distorts and blanks out the views and colours of the world outside. The ticket hall is a fortress of brickwork creating a cold, rather inhospitable atmosphere, which is not uplifting. Was it to do with cost constraints or the disposition of the architect for red brickwork? I think it was both.

The last but most understated platforms and canopies are the Stratford platforms and the administrative building. For me this is how a modern above-ground station should look. It is a well-engineered structure built to a tight budget, pared down to the essentials where the architect has skilfully modelled the proportion and scale of the modest structure. The roof overhang, the rhythm of the tapering profile of the cantilever beams, the orderly spacing of the welded cleat connections that support the roof and the alignment of the slender stanchions all bring harmony and balance to the space. The arrangement of grey ceramic tiled blockwork framing the stainless steel

seating block is simple and effective. Although most of the platform structure is either clad in grey-coloured panels or painted grey, it looks bright and cheerful, there is nothing drab. The façade of the long administrative building (which stands three storeys high adjacent to the western platform) looks suspiciously like concrete but it is not. It is patinated zinc that has been profiled to give the appearance of stack-bonded flush-jointed, stone sections. It was not the architect's preferred choice of surface finish but it has worked well and compliments the platforms and the terminus building. This is architecture of great merit, using a limited palette of materials and fine tuning and refining the bones of the structure.

The JLE has set new standards in underground station design and shown the public and LUL what a debt we owe the architects who worked on them. You will not see another Canary Wharf, Westminster, Canning Town or North Greenwich again because they were unique to the JLE and the developments surrounding them. Let us hope that we will see more cut-and-cover stations like Bermondsey, tunnelled stations like London Bridge and above-ground stations as good as Stratford.

Index

147